M000036446

For Stephen R. Haynes
Bonhoeffer scholar, dedicated disciple, esteemed friend
With gratitude

MORNINGS WITH
BONHOEFFER

100 REFLECTIONS ON THE CHRISTIAN LIFE

DONALD K. MCKIM

Abingdon Press / *Nashville*

MORNINGS WITH BONHOEFFER
100 REFLECTIONS ON THE CHRISTIAN LIFE

Copyright © 2018 by Donald McKim

Library of Congress Cataloging-in-Publication Data has been requested.

ISBN 978-1-5018-6481-0

Scripture quotations are taken from the New Revised Standard Version Bible, copyright © 1989 National Council of the Churches of Christ in the United States of America. Used by permission. All rights reserved worldwide. http://nrsvbibles.org/

Material for the time line drawn from *Christian History* magazine, issue #32, *Dietrich Bonhoeffer*, used with permission from ChristianHistoryInstitute.org.

18 19 20 21 22 23 24 25 26—10 9 8 7 6 5 4 3 2 1
MANUFACTURED IN THE UNITED STATES OF AMERICA

Contents

Preface

Through the years, I've had a passion to communicate theological insights to others, especially in the context of the church's life. One way I have tried to do this is through devotional books to introduce and interpret theologians by providing short, devotional reflections on a quotation from their writings. Thus *Coffee with Calvin: Daily Devotions* and *Moments with Martin Luther: 95 Daily Devotions* emerged.

Now it is Dietrich Bonhoeffer's turn. Bonhoeffer's language may be more directly understandable than Luther's and Calvin's since he is closer to us historically. But his thoughts are profound for Christian theology and for Christian living. My hope here is to interpret Bonhoeffer and reflect on the meaning and significance of his thoughts for our lives today in the church and as Christian disciples.

I first encountered a Dietrich Bonhoeffer book when I was a sophomore at Westminster College in Pennsylvania in 1968. On Sunday evenings, our Christian study group read and discussed Bonhoeffer's *The Cost of Discipleship*. I'd known about Bonhoeffer's life, but his classic book put forth the demand of Jesus to "Follow me" in direct and compelling ways. Bonhoeffer's book helped orient me to a life of discipleship and the meaning of the "costly grace" that obedience to Jesus Christ brings.

A few years later, I took a course on Bonhoeffer at Pittsburgh Theological Seminary with Dr. Arthur C. Cochrane, an expert on Bonhoeffer as he was on Karl Barth. This course introduced me to a range of Bonhoeffer's writings and the power of Bonhoeffer's theological witness in the midst of the evils being perpetrated by the Nazi regime in Germany.

When I taught theology in seminary, I always had students read Bonhoeffer's *Christ the Center* in courses on Christology. This pressed the question of how we understand Jesus Christ theologically, as the church has wrestled with this question through the centuries. But Bonhoeffer also asks the timeless question, "Who is Jesus Christ for us today?" This gives importance and immediacy to understanding Christ as a present reality who engages the world and each of us.

Bonhoeffer's thoughts are interconnected. Each theme in Bonhoeffer is related to other themes. This book of reflections does not try to present Bonhoeffer's theology as a coherent whole or to go into theological depth about the quotations presented for each reflection. Instead, the short reflections seek to present basic understandings and open visions for interpreting what Bonhoeffer's thoughts can mean for our Christian faith.

The reflections are divided into two main parts: "Believing as a Christian" and "Living as a Christian." Several themes make up each part. These are fluid categories, and there is no attempt to be thoroughly systematic in presenting the reflections in a specific order. The book can be used on a daily basis and read straight through, or it can be read at "random"—any time and in any order. Some suggestions about using the book follow here. The theological hope is that the Holy Spirit will be actively engaged in the reading and reflection on each piece—whenever and wherever!

I would like to thank folks at Abingdon Press, who have been collegially helpful with this project. Mary Catherine Dean, associate publisher and editor-in-chief, has been most gracious and supportive. Dawn L. Woods enthusiastically and encouragingly helped through the publication approval process, for which I am most appreciative. Susan Salley has been kind and efficient through the publication process. Thanks also to Christina Boys for sharing her excellent editorial skills and to Susan Cornell for her fine help as well. Brenda Smotherman has valuably worked on publicity and marketing.

As always, my work could not be done without the love of my family. My wonderful wife, LindaJo, is my loving partner in all things, bringing gladness and delight to our life together. Our son Stephen and his wife, Caroline, with Maddie, Annie, and Jack, bless our lives in incomparable ways; as do our son Karl and his wife, Lauren. For the deep goodness of family love, we rejoice.

Special thanks go to the interlibrary loan department of the Germantown Public Library. These neighbors have been unfailingly competent and friendly in securing interlibrary loan materials.

My thanks extend to all who have labored long to provide Bonhoeffer resources, especially those involved in the Dietrich Bonhoeffer Works in English project. Thanks to those who have written extensively on Bonhoeffer, especially on the works in the "Selected Resources for Further Reflection" section.

When I was an editor for Westminster John Knox Press, it was a joy to invite my friends Stephen R. Haynes and Lori Brandt Hale, two superb Bonhoeffer scholars, to write *Bonhoeffer for Armchair Theologians* with illustrations by Ron Hill. This, I believe, is the best short introduction to Bonhoeffer's life and thought available.

This book is dedicated to my friend, Steve Haynes. Steve is the Albert Bruce Curry Professor of Religious Studies at Rhodes College in Memphis and has been a firm friend for a long time. Though he describes himself as "more of a Bonhoeffer devotee than a Bonhoeffer scholar," he certainly is a Bonhoeffer scholar and has made a number of important contributions to Bonhoeffer scholarship. Steve is a deeply committed Presbyterian Church (USA) minister, a fine teacher with a pastor's heart, and a wonderful person who embodies Bonhoeffer's words: "Discipleship is joy." I am most grateful for our friendship.

My hope is this book will introduce readers to Dietrich Bonhoeffer. For those who already know him and his writing, I trust new insights on Bonhoeffer and from Bonhoeffer will be yours through these reflections.

Donald K. McKim
Germantown, Tennessee
February 1, 2018

Using This Book

This is a book of reflections on Christian faith based on quotations from Dietrich Bonhoeffer. The reflections are meant to explain Bonhoeffer's thoughts and open considerations on the meanings of Bonhoeffer's words for the church and for Christian life today. The quotations in each devotion are drawn from the volumes in the Dietrich Bonhoeffer Works from Fortress Press with volume and page number at the end of each quotation. A list of volumes used can be found in the "Selected Resources" section at the back of the book.

My article looking into Bonhoeffer's life and the events that shaped his thoughts can be found at www.abingdon press.com/MorningswithBonhoeffer.

This book can be used for group devotions in various gatherings, or it can be used for personal devotion and reflection.

Read. A Scripture passage or verse is found at the top of each page. The Scripture can be meditated upon before the reflection is read. These thoughts can be kept in mind as the reflection is read.

Since the writing for each reflection is compact, each sentence has meaning and can be a source for contemplation. Reading each sentence can be deliberate, and one can pause after each sentence to think about it.

Meditate. After the reflection is read, one can ask:

- What has Bonhoeffer said here?
- What do Bonhoeffer's thoughts mean for the life of the church?
- What do Bonhoeffer's thoughts mean for my life?
- What changes of attitude or actions are Bonhoeffer's words calling me (or us) toward?
- What are practical ways Bonhoeffer's thoughts can be put into practice in the church community? In my own life?

Pray. Incorporate what has emerged in your reading and meditation into a prayer. Pray for God's Holy Spirit to take this experience and lead into what God would have you be and do.

Act. Put into practice what the reflection points toward by acting in ways that reorient your present directions in life or that open new directions for service and action.

⌐⌐⌐

The title of each reflection can serve as a key phrase to bring important dimensions of the reflections to mind. You can review the contents and summarize what each reflection has meant to you, perhaps in the space at the end of each one.

If you keep a journal, a summary of the reflection/experience and what it means to you can be recorded. These summaries can be reviewed at various times in the future.

You can also consult works in the "Selected Resources for Further Reflection" section to pursue further readings by and about Bonhoeffer.

Part 1

Believing as a Christian

Christian Beliefs

1

Scripture Is God's Own Word

What is Holy Scripture? It is God's own word, in which, through the prophets and the apostles, he proclaims to me and to the church-community that Jesus Christ is God's Son and my sav[ior]. (14:785)

⌐⌐⌐

For Dietrich Bonhoeffer, as for all Protestants, Holy Scripture is the Word of God. The biblical canon—the books of the Old and New Testaments—is God's revelation. In Scripture, God communicates God's own self to us humans. Without the Scriptures, we would have no way of knowing God. We cannot peel back the clouds and look upon God in heaven! If we are to know who God is, it is God who has to "make the first move." God must reveal who God is if we are ever to come to a knowledge of God.

We believe God has spoken in the Scriptures. The Bible is "God's own word," says Bonhoeffer, given to us "through the prophets and the apostles." The biblical Scriptures are given through human beings who witness to what God has said and done.

The Bible is given to the "church-community," as Bonhoeffer said, and "to me." It proclaims a message: "that

5

Jesus Christ is God's Son and my savior." This is the purpose of the Bible. Scripture points us to what God has done in sending Jesus Christ, God's eternal Son. Jesus died on the cross so our sin against God can be forgiven. Jesus is our savior. When we believe in Jesus Christ we have "eternal life" (John 3:16).

Scripture gives "good news"—a word from God proclaiming God's love for us and the way of salvation, how we can live as God's people and be in a relationship of trust and love with God. We read God's Word, hear the Scriptures proclaimed, and live in faith as God's people.

2

The Mirror of the Creator

> Humankind is here the final work of God's self-glorifi-
> cation. The world is created for God, for God's honor
> alone, and humankind is the most precious receptacle,
> the very mirror of the Creator. It is totally for the sake
> of God's glory and honor as Creator that everything
> comes to pass. (3:72)

⌐⌐⌐

Genesis 1 tells us of God creating the heavens and the earth. God is the sovereign creator of all things.

The climax and completion of creation is the creation of humankind. God's good work of creation is expressed most clearly when God created humans in the divine image: "So God created humankind in his image" (Genesis 1:26).

Bonhoeffer commented on humankind in his theological work, *Creation and Fall*. He wrote, "Humankind is here the final work of God's self-glorification. The world is created for God, for God's honor alone, and humankind is the most precious receptacle, the very mirror of the Creator. It is totally for the sake of God's glory and honor as Creator that everything comes to pass."

God's creation brings honor and glory to the creator. God's honor permeates the universe and is displayed on earth. The "most precious" place where God's glory is received is in humans. Human beings are "the very mirror of the Creator." We "reflect" God as a mirror since we are created in the "image" of God. When people see us, they should be reminded of God—not by how we look but by who we are and what we do. We live for God's glory! Are we a "mirror" of our Creator to others?

God creates and then sustains and guides the creation so it is "for the sake of God's glory and honor" that all things happen. Let us rejoice and reflect our good Creator!

3

No Longer Loving the Other

This [the fall] means the human being no longer regards
the other person with love. Instead one person sees the
other in terms of their being over against each other;
each sees the other as divided from himself or herself.
(3:122)

⌒⌒⌒

There is a sad situation in human life. We see it every time
we read the daily news. The bad news is the human condition—who humans are and what they do.

Bonhoeffer wrote a powerful book, *Creation and Fall*, in
which he interpreted the early chapters of Genesis, which tell
not only of God's creation of humanity but also what humans
did—which has affected human nature ever since.

God created humans to live in God's image, to live in
freedom and obedience to their Creator. But the stories in
Genesis 3 describe what theologians such as Bonhoeffer call
"the fall" of humanity. Instead of obeying God, humans
rebel against God. They want to be "like God" (Genesis 3:5).
Instead of putting God, from whom humans draw life, at
the center of life, humans turn in upon themselves (an image
Luther often used) and put themselves at the center of their

existence. Humans have fallen away from God, seeking to become their own creator.

The result is the relationship of trust and obedience between God and humans is lost. By being divided from the creator, humans also become divided against themselves. As Bonhoeffer writes, "This [the fall] means the human being no longer regards the other person with love. Instead one person sees the other in terms of their being over against each other; each sees the other as divided from himself or herself."

The daily news shows people against each other, even violently so. Love is not our natural inclination. Only God can help. God help us!

4

The Center of the Gospel

The center of the gospel—"redemption" is the word around which everything turns. (8:422)

━ ━ ━

On June 6, 1944, the day of the Allied landing on Normandy, Bonhoeffer wrote to his friend Eberhard Bethge from prison. He mentioned the *Daily Text*, a series of biblical texts for each day of the year. On this day, the texts were Psalm 38:4 and Ephesians 1:7. Bonhoeffer said these texts call us to "the center of the gospel—'redemption' is the word around which everything turns."

Psalm 38 is the psalmist's prayer for healing. He confesses his sin and says, "My iniquities have gone over my head; they weigh like a burden too heavy for me" (Psalm 38:4). The whole psalm pleads for God's help, concluding with the appeal, "O my God do not be far from me; make haste to help me, O Lord, my salvation" (Psalm 38:21b-22).

This plea for help and healing is met by God's coming near to all people in the person of God's Son, Jesus Christ. As Paul said, "In him we have redemption through his blood, the forgiveness of our trespasses, according to the riches of his grace" (Ephesians 1:7).

Redemption—that word is the center of the gospel, "the word around which everything turns," wrote Bonhoeffer. God has sent Jesus Christ to die on the cross, so that through him, sinners can be redeemed. In Christ is redemption—just what the psalmist and all of us need! By God's grace in Jesus Christ, our sin is forgiven, our lives are made new, and our burdens are lifted—for which the psalmist prayed. The good news of the gospel is liberation! The power of sin is broken, and we are free to serve God in Christ and to serve all other children of God. Redemption!

5

The Holy Spirit Brings Christ

The Holy Spirit brings Christ to individuals (Romans 8:14; Ephesians 2:22) and establishes community among them. (2 Corinthians 13:13; Philippians 2:1) (1:139)

⮜⮜⮜

The work of the Holy Spirit is mysterious. The New Testament says much of what the Spirit does. But unless we stop to think and observe, we may miss what the Spirit is doing.

Bonhoeffer cites a number of Scripture passages to remind us that one of the primary works of the Holy Spirit is to bring Christ into our lives. Paul wrote that "all who are led by the Spirit of God are children of God" (Romans 8:14). We become "children of God" by faith, and faith is given to us as a gift of God through the Holy Spirit (Ephesians 2:8). We know Jesus Christ today because God's Spirit has been at work within us.

But the Spirit does more. Bonhoeffer notes that along with bringing Christ to individuals, the Spirit "establishes community among them." The Spirit brings together all who have faith in Jesus Christ as their Lord and Savior. This is what the Apostles' Creed calls the "communion of saints," or the "church." Bonhoeffer's doctoral dissertation was called *Sanctorum Communio*, "the communion of saints." The church community we see around us as we worship and in which we participate as people who confess their faith in Jesus Christ is established by Christ's action through the work of the Holy Spirit. The Spirit creates the community of those who have responded to Christ's call to be his disciples.

Our faith is strengthened when we realize we become children of God by the Spirit's work in bringing Christ to us. The church, as the work of the Spirit, is the community where our identity as Christ's disciples is expressed and lived!

6

Justification and Sanctification

Justification is the new creation of the new person, and
sanctification is the preservation and protection of that
person until the day of Jesus Christ. (4:260)

⌒⌒⌒

An important image to describe salvation is justification.
Paul writes that "since we are justified by faith, we have
peace with God through our Lord Jesus Christ" (Romans
5:1). Bonhoeffer articulates his Lutheran tradition in which
justification refers to "the new creation of the new person."
Justification gives us a new standing of being (declared) righteous before God, based on the death of Jesus Christ. Those
justified by faith in Jesus Christ are incorporated into the
body of Christ, the "church community." For Bonhoeffer, justification, like baptism, is a "once and for all," unrepeatable
event. Justification means we are "in Christ," we are a "new
creation" (2 Corinthians 5:17). Now our sin is forgiven, our
past is over and gone, and we are liberated from the power of
sin to condemn us in God's sight. For Bonhoeffer, Christ has
obeyed the law of God on our behalf, and through faith, we
receive Christ's righteousness as being for us. In justification,
we are "set right" with God. We are saved.

Bonhoeffer says *sanctification* describes the "preservation and safekeeping unto the day of Jesus Christ" of those who are justified. By God's Holy Spirit, the justified grow in faith throughout life and are enabled to stay close to Jesus Christ. Now we are continually promised God's present and future action through the Spirit to help us fulfill God's will in our daily lives. The Spirit preserves us in faith and, like Noah's ark, preserves us through the floods of life and brings us safely to our ultimate salvation (1 Thessalonians 5:23; 1 Peter 1:5).

Praise to God who saves us and preserves us in Jesus Christ!

7

Forgiving the Sins of the World

The world exhausts its rage on the body of Jesus Christ. But the martyred one forgives the world its sins. Thus reconciliation takes place. *Ecce homo* ["Here is the man!" (John 19:5)]. (6:83)

⌒⌒⌒

Jesus Christ brings the reconciliation of the world to God. As Paul proclaims about Christ: "through him God was pleased to reconcile to himself all things, whether on earth or in heaven, by making peace through the blood of his cross" (Colossians 1:20). We cannot imagine a greater act of God on our behalf—all through Jesus Christ.

Bonhoeffer emphasized that God takes on our sin and forgives the sins of the world in Jesus Christ. Jesus brings reconciliation between sinful, guilty humans and the God who loves us. Bonhoeffer wrote, "The world exhausts its rage on the body of Jesus Christ. But the martyred one forgives the world its sins. Thus reconciliation takes place. *Ecce homo*." Despite all that sin could do to Jesus—even bringing his death—Jesus forgives: "Father, forgive them" (Luke 23:34). Jesus absorbs human guilt and the suffering guilt has brought. In Jesus, holiness absorbs sin; love overcomes

17

hate. The world is not overcome by destruction. It is forgiven through reconciliation. This is what theologians call "atonement." God and humanity are "at-one" by the death of Jesus Christ on the cross. Here is "the Lamb of God who takes away the sin of the world!" (John 1:29).

The only one who can bring this reconciliation is Jesus Christ, the eternal Son of God who became a human being to die for us. Jesus took our sins upon himself. This is the gospel message to liberate our lives from the power of sin. We are forgiven. Now we have peace with God. In Jesus, God shows overflowing love for us!

8

The Meaning of the Easter Message

The meaning of the *Easter* message is that God is the death of death; God lives and so Christ lives also; death could not hold Christ against the superior power of God. God pronounced a decree against death, destroyed it, and resurrected Jesus Christ. (10:488)

⇀⇀⇀

Some have called 1 Corinthians 15 the "spinal cord of the New Testament." It is Paul's great chapter on resurrection. Paul proclaimed the resurrection of Jesus Christ and our own resurrection as believers in Christ. All the future comes to this: "If Christ has not been raised, your faith is futile and you are still in your sins" (1 Corinthians 15:17).

But because Christ is raised, the power of death has been defeated. The power of sin is broken now, and resurrection life awaits. This is the Easter promise. As Bonhoeffer put it in a sermon, "The meaning of the *Easter* message is that God is the death of death; God lives and so Christ lives also; death could not hold Christ against the superior power of God. God pronounced a decree against death, destroyed it, and resurrected Jesus Christ."

Jesus Christ is alive! Death could not hold him. Christ is raised by the power of God. As we confess in the Apostles' Creed, "the third day he rose again from the dead." This opens an eternal future for the dead, who will be raised, and for us who are living to know we have an eternal future freed from sin and alive forever in Christ Jesus.

Bonhoeffer's focus on God's providing "the death of death" in the resurrection of Christ gives hope. This Easter message is a message for our lives every day. We can live in assurance that the worst that can be done to us—death—is conquered in Christ!

9

The Nearby God

Remember, I am with you...that is the Easter message,
not the distant, but the nearby God, that is Easter.
(10:491)

⌒⌒⌒

When Bonhoeffer served as a pastoral assistant in
a Lutheran congregation in Barcelona, Spain, he
preached on the first Sunday after Easter, April 15, 1928.
His sermon addressed a basic human question: Can we walk
with God?

The great gulf between God and humans is caused by sin.
This is the story Bonhoeffer described in his book *Creation
and Fall*. Genesis 3 tells of humanity's rebellion against
God and that Adam and Eve—representing all of us—were
expelled from the garden of Eden. The relationship of loving
trust they had with God since their creation was broken. Sin
did its worst the day Jesus hung on the cross. The distance
between sinful humans and their creator could not be greater
than on Good Friday.

But Bonhoeffer told the congregation there was a divine
response to this sin. There was a day when humanity was
filled with divine grace: Easter! This was the day Jesus Christ

was raised from the dead. Now Jesus is with us, always (Matthew 28:20). Bonhoeffer proclaimed, "Remember, I am with you . . . that is the Easter message, not the distant, but the nearby God, that is Easter."

Now the distance between us and God has been overcome. Now our relationship of loving trust is restored. Jesus Christ has reconciled us with God, our sin is forgiven, and now God is with us. Now we can walk with God because God is "the nearby God." God is with us in Jesus Christ.

This Easter message is for the whole world to hear and believe! Since God is nearby—with us in Jesus Christ—we can keep our eyes open to see where we encounter Jesus among us.

1 0

The Christian and the Worldly Become One in Christ

Just as in Jesus Christ God and humanity became one, so through Christ what is Christian and what is worldly become one in the action of the Christian. (6:238)

‿‿‿

Bonhoeffer's theology focused on Jesus Christ and what God did in Christ for the sake of the world. The words of John the Baptist expressed who Jesus was and what Jesus would do. John said, "Here is the Lamb of God who takes away the sin of the world!" (John 1:29). Jesus, the Son of God, offered himself in his death for the forgiveness of sins to take away "the sin of the world." This unites God and humanity through what Jesus Christ did for the sake of the world God loves (John 3:16).

Bonhoeffer emphasized the concrete nature of what Jesus did—he lived and died in the real world, with real people, as a real person. Jesus' life and work was for the sake of the world and all people.

This carries over into what Christians do today. We serve Jesus Christ in the world. Our mission and ministries of discipleship in following Jesus take place in the here and now. Christians are the most "worldly" of people! Why? Because Jesus Christ became a human person and died for the sin of this world. Bonhoeffer wrote, "Just as in Jesus Christ God and humanity became one, so through Christ what is Christian and what is worldly become one in the action of the Christian."

Critics of Christianity have said Christianity offers "pie in the sky by and by." They see Christianity as an "other-worldly faith." But the emphasis of the Gospel we proclaim is that "what is Christian and what is worldly" are united in us—because of Jesus Christ!

1 1

The Ascended Christ Is Close to Us

He is close to us in his church, in his Word, in his sacrament, in love among the brethren. Here he comforts us who are abandoned; here he soothes our homesickness ever anew; here he takes us who are estranged from God, who are in barren, empty places, who don't know the way, who are alone, and makes us joyful in his Christly presence.... That is the joy of the believing church in its unseen, heavenly Lord. (12:469)

≈≈≈

A scension Day is the fortieth day of Easter, the day the church remembers the ascension of Jesus into heaven (Acts 1:6-11). Ascension Day is very important, even though it often passes nearly unnoticed in our churches and in our lives of faith. Bonhoeffer preached an Ascension Day sermon on May 25, 1933, in Berlin in which he spoke movingly of the joy of Christ's ascension.

He noted that Martin Luther once commented that while Christ was on earth, Jesus was far away from us—limited to one place. But now that Christ is ascended to heaven, he is very close to us all the time. Christ is close to us in the church, through Word and sacrament, and in the love the church community shares. Every day!

Then, movingly, Bonhoeffer said that here on earth, Jesus "comforts us who are abandoned; here he soothes our homesickness ever anew; here he takes us who are estranged from God, who are in barren, empty places, who don't know the way, who are alone, and makes us joyful in his Christly presence.... That is the joy of the believing church in its unseen, heavenly Lord."

We can be grateful that Jesus "ascended into heaven" (Apostles' Creed). Now he is close to us to bring us joy—no matter what our sorrow or situation!

1 2

God Has a Purpose

God is concerned not only with the nations, but has a purpose for every community no matter how small, every friendship, every marriage, every family. And in this sense God also has a purpose for the *church.* (1:119)

⌒⌒⌒

Throughout the Bible, God calls people. God calls groups of people and individual persons.

God calls people to carry out God's purposes in the world. Those who respond to God's call are enlisted in God's service. They devote themselves to what God calls them to do to accomplish the divine will in the world. God chose the people of Israel and said, "I... will be your God, and you shall be my people'" (Leviticus 26:12). Jesus called his disciples: "Follow me and I will make you fish for people" (Mark 1:17). God works in and through people to accomplish God's will in the world.

Bonhoeffer recognized this when he wrote that "God is concerned not only with the nations, but has a purpose for every community no matter how small, every friendship,

27

every marriage, every family. And in this sense God also has a purpose for the *church*."

All groups and individuals called by God receive God's blessings but also have responsibilities to carry out God's will and purposes. Communities and all persons must repent of their sins against God, believe, and carry out God's word according to God's call. Collectively, every community stands before God to be faithful—or unfaithful—to the call God gives. Individuals, in all our relationships—friendship, marriage, and families—have our decisions about ways to live out the purposes for which God has called us. The church's great purpose is to be the community in which Christ exists and that carries out Christ's purposes to meet human needs. Live out God's purpose!

1 3

Faith Believes Only in God

> This is faith: it does not rely on itself or on favorable seas, favorable conditions; it does not rely on its own strength or on other people's strength, but believes only and alone in God, whether or not there is a storm. …Lord, make this faith strong in us who have little faith! (12:460)

━━━

The story of Jesus quieting the storm is an enacted story of faith and its challenges (Matthew 8:23-27).

The disciples were in a boat with Jesus. A storm arose, and the boat was swamped with waves. Jesus was asleep. The disciples woke him in fear. Jesus asked, "Why are you afraid, you of little faith?" Then Jesus rebuked the winds and the sea was "dead calm." The disciples were amazed.

Bonhoeffer preached a sermon on this story on January 15, 1933, in Berlin during a time of great tension. This was shortly before Hitler came to power, and there were many political fears.

But Bonhoeffer's message was that we can have faith instead of fear. "This is faith," he said: "It does not rely on itself or on favorable seas, favorable conditions; it does not rely on its own strength or on other people's strength, but believes only and alone in God, whether or not there is a storm....Lord, make this faith strong in us who have little faith!"

Faith is trust. It is trust in Jesus, even when he seems to be asleep in the boat. Through all conditions of life—in calm seas or dangerous seas, faith trusts in Jesus. It does not rely on its own strength. Faith believes only in God. Faith overcomes fear because God saves those who are perishing. We are people of "little faith." But Jesus is with us. He can calm our fears. He gives us faith.

1 4

Lord of the Ages

> The Lord of the ages is God. The turning point of the
> ages is Christ. The true spirit of the age [*Zeitgeist*] is
> the Holy Spirit. (10:531)

꙲꙲꙲

Bonhoeffer's great-grandfather was Karl August von Hase. He was a distinguished church historian who wrote the *History of the Christian Church.* A theme of that book was "The Lord of the ages is God. The turning point of the ages is Christ. The true spirit of the age [*Zeitgeist*] is the Holy Spirit."

This trinitarian description provides a theological view of history. Though we live our life histories one day at a time, in the great vision of history presented in the Bible, we acknowledge that God is "the Lord of the ages." God is the Lord of history who guides history and is the One to whom all history will ultimately bow.

Jesus Christ is the "turning point of the ages." Christ has come, and the world is changed. Now salvation is possible. Now the decisive story in history is the story of Jesus Christ and the redemption he brings to the world.

The Holy Spirit is "the true spirit of the age." This meant, for Bonhoeffer, that despite all the tragedies, miseries, and sin in the world—which he saw in the diabolical evil of Nazism—God's Spirit is the "true spirit of the age" because God's Spirit is at work in the world through all sin and evil.

This is the future vision of Revelation when the "loud voices in heaven" proclaim, "The kingdom of the world has become the kingdom of our Lord and of his Messiah, and he will reign forever and ever" (Revelation 11:15). This vision pulls us forward in this age and every age as we anticipate the final triumph of God's reign!

Jesus Christ

1 5

Miracle of Miracles

No priest, no theologian stood at the cradle of
Bethlehem. And yet all Christian theology finds its origin in the miracle of miracles, that God became human.
...*Theologia sacra* [sacred theology]—it originates in
prayerful kneeling before the mystery of the divine
child in the stable. (15:528)

⌒⌒⌒

Bonhoeffer was a theologian. He taught in a university,
and his work, from beginning to end, was that of a theologian who sought to explain the Christian faith. This was an
important calling that was vital for the church.

Yet in his "Theological Letter on Christmas" to pastors
in December 1939, Bonhoeffer powerfully wrote, "No priest,
no theologian stood at the cradle of Bethlehem. And yet all
Christian theology finds its origin in the miracle of miracles,
that God became human.... *Theologia sacra* [sacred theol-
ogy]—it originates in prayerful kneeling before the mystery
of the divine child in the stable."

The beginning of all Christian theology is faith. It is
"kneeling before the mystery of the divine child in the stable"—Jesus Christ. Bonhoeffer's theology was centered

in Jesus Christ, who is "the miracle of miracles." In Jesus Christ, "God became human." This is the astounding message of the Christian faith! This is the unique gospel message the church proclaims. From this "good news," all Christian faith and Christian theology emerge and develop.

We always need to go back to the most basic, most important faith conviction: God became human in Jesus Christ. Our faith leads us to seek understanding—of Christ and all theology. But all our intellectual quests and questions, like the shepherds, ultimately come to the "cradle of Bethlehem." There we prayerfully kneel before the Christ child who is God with us—God became a human being for our sakes. Praise God for coming to us in Jesus Christ!

16

Who Is Jesus Christ?

Who is Jesus Christ? Jesus Christ is completely God
and completely human being in one person. As such he
is the mediator between God and me and is my savior.
1 Timothy 2:5. (14:799)

⇌⇌⇌

As part of his instruction to seminarians at Finkenwalde,
Bonhoeffer presented "a confirmation plan" for teaching the Christian faith to children who were to be confirmed
in the church. Based on student notes by Eberhard Bethge, we
have Bonhoeffer's thoughts about what was most important
for young people who are becoming members of the church
to know.

Here we have a very succinct answer to the important
question: "Who is Jesus Christ?" The person of Jesus Christ is
central to Christianity. During its early centuries, the church
debated various ways of expressing its faith to Jesus' question
to Peter: "Who do you say that I am?" (Matthew 16:15).

Bonhoeffer's answer conveys the church's conviction:
"Jesus Christ is completely God and completely human being
in one person." Jesus Christ is the "divine-human" being one
person with two natures, as the church came to express it. He

is the Son of God and also the Christ of God (John 1:1, 14; 6:68-69). Jesus Christ is the eternal *logos*, or word of God who became a human being to embody God's love.

Jesus Christ is "the mediator between God and me and is my savior (1 Timothy 2:5)," said Bonhoeffer. Through his death on the cross, Jesus Christ is the mediator between God and humanity. In his death, he brought reconciliation and forgiveness for the sin of humanity.

Bonhoeffer links the person and the work of Christ. Jesus is mediator because of who he is: "completely God and completely human in one person." His death can save us from our sins. Jesus Christ is "my savior."

1 7

Jesus Christ Is Reconciliation

Love thus denotes what God does to human beings to
overcome the disunion in which they lived. This deed is
called Christ, it is called reconciliation. (6:336)

⸺⸺⸺

The Bible says "God is love" (1 John 4:8, 16) and that
"God proves his love for us in that while we still were
sinners Christ died for us" (Romans 5:8). Love is who God is
and what God does.

In the New Testament, the God of love reaches out to
human beings by becoming a person in Jesus Christ. Jesus
personified God's love in all he said and did. His teachings
were to "love one another" (John 13:34; 15:12). His actions
were to suffer and die to bring forgiveness and reconciliation
between sinful humans and the God who loves them.

Bonhoeffer described this when he wrote that "love thus
denotes what God does to human beings to overcome the
disunion in which they lived. This deed is called Christ, it
is called reconciliation." Reconciliation comes through the
cross of Jesus Christ (2 Corinthians 5:18). Jesus' death brings
peace (Romans 5:1) and overcomes the break in the relationship of love, which our choice to "go our own way" in life

has brought each of us. Reconciliation brings two persons together.

Jesus Christ is the reconciliation that transforms our lives. We receive salvation, the fullness of life God desires us to have. God loves us, and in Christ, by the power of the Holy Spirit, we now love others in ways not possible before when we were self-centered instead of God-centered and other-centered. As 1 John puts it, "We love because he first loved us" (1 John 4:19).

We love God and others because God has first reached out to love us in Christ. Jesus Christ is reconciliation. Praise God's reconciling love!

1 8

Christ Conquers Death

Death reveals that the world is not as it should be but
that it stands in need of redemption. Christ alone is the
conquering of death. (16:207)

⌐⌐⌐

During the years Bonhoeffer led an underground seminary at Finkenwalde to prepare ministers in the midst of
the Nazi regime and during fighting by the Germans against
the Allied forces, friends, pastors, and students were killed. In
his circular letter of August 15, 1941, Bonhoeffer reported on
the death of three of the "brothers" of the seminary family.

Bonhoeffer went on to write about death. He saw God
and the devil as "engaged in battle in the world" and that
"the devil also has a say in death." Bonhoeffer did not believe
we can say "God wills it" but rather we should realize
another reality: "God does not will it." For "death reveals
that the world is not as it should be but that it stands in need
of redemption. Christ alone is the conquering of death."
This is the word we need. The world's redemption rests in
Jesus Christ. He redeems by conquering death—the result of
human sin.

God's will can conquer evil and human sin—in Christ. Wrote Bonhoeffer, "God wills the conquering of death through the death of Jesus Christ. Only in the cross and resurrection of Jesus Christ has death been drawn into God's power, and it must now serve God's own aims." It is only "a living faith in Jesus Christ, who died and rose for us, that is able to cope profoundly with death."

Death's power, so apparently real to us, has truly been defeated in Jesus Christ. This is our ultimate hope and our salvation. This is the reality to which we cling, even in times of profound sadness.

1 9

Christ Incognito

In being humiliated, Christ, the God-human, enters of his own free will into the world of sin and death. He enters there in such a way as to conceal himself [there], so that he is no longer recognizable visibly as the God-human. He comes among us humans not in [Godly form] but rather incognito, as a beggar among beggars, an outcast among outcasts; he comes among sinners as the one without sin, but also as a sinner among sinners. (12:356)

——

Jesus Christ is central in Bonhoeffer's theology. His 1933 lectures on Christology have come to us through student notes. They focus on the ultimate mystery of the Trinity: that the eternal God should become a human person in Jesus Christ (Philippians 2:5-8).

God is the God of glory, the creator and Lord of all. But God is glorified not by great displays of power but by becoming a human in the man, Jesus. He is the "God-human" who freely enters into the world of "sin and death," taking on human flesh. God glorifies the human, those who will share eternal life with the "three-in-one" God.

Jesus Christ does not enter the world with great displays of power. Instead, "he enters there in such a way as to conceal himself [there], so that he is no longer recognizable visibly as the God-human. He comes among us humans not in [Godly form] but rather incognito, as a beggar among beggars, an outcast among outcasts; he comes among sinners as the one without sin, but also as a sinner among sinners."

"Christ incognito" is the way of Jesus among us—as a beggar and outcast, as sinless but as a "sinner among sinners." This is where we find Jesus Christ today, in poor and marginalized people who, like us, need Jesus.

2 0

Jesus: Being for Others

Jesus's "being-for-others" is the experience of transcendence!...Faith is participating in this being of Jesus. ...Our relationship to God is a new life in "being there for others," through participation in the being of Jesus. The transcendent is not the infinite, unattainable tasks, but the neighbor within reach in any given situation. God in human form! (8:501)

〜〜〜

From prison on August 3, 1944, Bonhoeffer wrote to Eberhard Bethge and enclosed an outline for a book he wanted to write. One section would deal with "Who is God?"

A famous segment of this part included the quotations above. These were key expressions of Bonhoeffer's understanding of Jesus Christ, expressed in 1933 lectures and in his conception of ethics. These led to a famous characterization of Bonhoeffer's view of Jesus as "the man for others." Now this is rendered "the human being for others."

It is Jesus' "being-for-others" that marks transcendence. God is not remote but rather experienced by faith as one participates in this "being of Jesus." New life comes to us as we are "being there for others," reaching out to them in self-giving love. The transcendent is experienced by "being there" for "the neighbor within reach in any given situation. God is in human form!" Jesus is not an abstraction; he is a real human who met the needs of others in everyday situations. This ultimately led Jesus to the cross.

Jesus' followers, those who know the "costly grace" of discipleship—the church—are committed to "being for others" too. The church can only truly be the church when it is "for others." This is life with Christ. The church by speech and action is "Christ existing as community." We enter into Christ's ministries to the poor and suffering. For Bonhoeffer, this also meant standing against the evils of Nazism.

2 1

Christ the Center

> What is most precious in Christianity is Jesus Christ
> himself.... Christ is the center and power of the Bible,
> of the church, of theology, but also of humanity, reason,
> justice, and culture. To Christ everything must return;
> only under Christ's protection can it live. (6:341)

⊸⊸⊸

The image of "center" is important for Bonhoeffer.
God set the tree of the knowledge of good and evil
"in the middle of the garden" of Eden (Genesis 3:3). Adam
and Eve were not permitted to eat of it. They had a boundary.
But they disobeyed God, transgressed the boundary, and the
result was the fall into sin. Humans are now "turned in upon
themselves" (Luther), and we make ourselves the "center" of
our world. We know no "center" outside ourselves.

But in the midst of the sinful world, there is the cross of
Jesus Christ. This is the "most precious" thing in Christianity,
said Bonhoeffer. By his cross and reconciliation, Christ brings
the world to God in Christ. In Jesus Christ, a new center is
established—not the centeredness of sinfulness, but Christ
the center. Jesus Christ is the one in whom "all things hold
together" (Colossians 1:17).

This is the key for Bonhoeffer: "Christ is the center and power of the Bible, of the church, of theology, but also of humanity, reason, justice, and culture. To Christ everything must return; only under Christ's protection can it live." Jesus Christ is the source of life through which all things can live. He is the central reality of the universe, holding all things together by his power. He is the truth and the power of all things—Scripture, church, theology, justice and culture, and of humanity itself. Christ is the center of the life of the world! Christ is the center of our lives!

Church

2 2

Church Is the Act of God

Church, however, is *the church that is already actually established in Christ!* The church is there through [the] act of God, and has not been made by human beings! (11:306)

⌐⌐⌐

We often take the church for granted. Sunday morning comes, and it is the time to assemble for worship with sisters and brothers in Christ in our local congregation. Church is part of our routine. We participate in church, and we participate in other organizations and activities throughout our week. Church is "different" than the other groups. But why?

In Bonhoeffer's lecture on "The Nature of the Church," according to student notes, he said, "Church, however, is *the church that is already actually established in Christ!* The church is there through [the] act of God, and has not been made by human beings!" This puts church in its best perspective for us.

Our local congregations gain their lives from Jesus Christ and from the whole company of the "communion of saints"—the churches throughout the world. All these church communities have been established in Jesus Christ. We all receive life from him. The church is "the body of Christ," and we are reminded that in the church "there is one body and one Spirit" in which we are united (Ephesians 4:3-4).

Ultimately, the church is here, as Bonhoeffer said, "by the act of God." It has "not been made by human beings." This sets the church apart from all other groups. The church is an act of God in Jesus Christ. We are part of the church community because we have been called by God, saved by God's grace in Christ. The church is the only group in which you have to confess you are not worthy to be a member! God graciously gives us church, established in Christ!

2 3

Christ Existing as Church Community

> The church is the presence of Christ in the same way
> that Christ is the presence of God. The New Testament
> knows a form of revelation, "Christ existing as church-
> community." (1:140–41)

⌐⌐⌐

The Holy Spirit brings Christ to us. All those who receive Christ by the power of the Spirit are joined together in the church, which is the "body of Christ." As Paul wrote to the Corinthians, "You are the body of Christ and individually members of it" (1 Corinthians 12:27).

Bonhoeffer believed people created by God are created in human community, so human existence is best understood in relation to social relations, or "sociality." Bonhoeffer speaks of the "church-community" as the collective body of Christians who are called by God, who live as followers of Jesus Christ in discipleship, and who are drawn together in community by the Holy Spirit.

The church community is crucial. It is so important that Bonhoeffer says, "The church is the presence of Christ in the same way that Christ is the presence of God." Paul, said Bonhoeffer, frequently identified Jesus Christ with the church community of his disciples (1 Corinthians 3:16; 12:12). Christ is present in the church community, and the church community is united with and "in Christ" (2 Corinthians 5:17). Thus, for Bonhoeffer, "the New Testament knows a form of revelation, 'Christ existing as church-community.'"

This means there is no "solitary Christianity." Believers in Christ cannot live apart from the church community. Being part of the church is not an "option" for believers, it is an absolute necessity! Members of the church community are actively with and for each other in the body of Christ. We are united in Christ as a "collective person"—since Christ exists as church community. The church lives out the love and service to others Jesus taught and showed us.

2 4

Christian Community Is a Reality in Christ

> Christian community is not an ideal we have to realize,
> but rather a reality created by God in Christ in which
> we may participate. (5:38)

⌐⌐⌐

Sometimes we take the church for granted. It is part of our lives. We realize the church is the Christian community into which God has called us and where our service to God in Jesus Christ is strengthened and encouraged.

The Christian community is God's gift to us in Christ. It is different from all other groups because it is "a reality created by God in Christ in which we may participate," said Bonhoeffer. This is the pure grace of being part of the church. We do not have to struggle and work to "create church." The church is not, noted Bonhoeffer, "an ideal we have to realize." The church is prior to our participation in it. The Christian community is grounded and strengthened and given promises in Jesus Christ alone. These are present and are always with us. We live from the grace given by Christ through life together in the Christian community. This enables us to serve Christ in mission and ministry (1 Corinthians 12:27-31). God blesses our efforts in the community to live for others and be followers of Jesus Christ. Christ and church go together. Christ exists now in and through the Christian community, the "body of Christ" (1 Corinthians 12:27).

So the church—despite its failings and our own failings as members of the church—is God's gracious gift to us. The church is created as the community in Jesus Christ where Christ is present. Through the power of the Holy Spirit, we use the gifts we have received to be followers of Jesus who love the world for which Christ died.

2 5

Community of Sinners

The community of saints as the community of penitent sinners is held together by the unity of the body
of Christ. In the church, as in any other community,
people repent both for their own sin and for that of the
collective person of the community. (1:214)

⌐⌐⌐

Sometimes we see a bumper sticker that says: "Christians
are not perfect; only forgiven."

We Christians know that though our sin is forgiven
by Jesus Christ through his death on the cross, Christians
still sin. A famous expression of Martin Luther's is that the
Christian is "at the same time justified and a sinner." Sin is
a part of our lives as Christians, and we seek God's forgiveness over and over. We know the experience of the psalmist:
"Happy are those whose transgression is forgiven, whose sin
is covered" (Psalm 32:1).

The church is a "community of saints" but also a "community of penitent sinners," says Bonhoeffer. It is "held
together by the unity of the body of Christ." Only the Spirit
of God, who unites the church together as the body of Christ

where Christ exists as the church community, can bind forgiven sinners together.

The church is a community of sinners. But we are "penitent sinners." That is, we seek forgiveness for our sins. We repent or turn from sin when we receive God's forgiveness. In faith we pray for forgiveness and repentance for our sins and the sins of others. As Bonhoeffer says, church people "repent both for their own sin and for that of the collective person of the community." We pray for God's forgiveness of the sins of the church as a whole and the sins of our own lives. We pray on behalf of others as well as on our own behalf: God be merciful to the community of sinners!

2 6

Sisters and Brothers Through Christ

One is a brother or sister to another only through Jesus Christ. I am a brother or sister to another person through what Jesus Christ has done for me and to me; others have become brothers and sisters to me through what Jesus Christ has done for them and to them.... Our community consists solely in what Christ has done to both of us. (5:34)

⇌⇌⇌

When Paul wrote to the Philippian church, he referred to this congregation as "brothers and sisters" (Philippians 1:14). Those who share a common life together in the church are "related" to each other by their common relationship of faith in Jesus Christ.

In *Life Together*, Bonhoeffer explains that Christian community—one person with another—comes only through Jesus Christ. This relationship is found in the context of the church community here and now and extends into eternity. Our "sister and brother" relationship is established only through what Jesus Christ has done in his life, death, and resurrection for each one of us.

We are "a brother or sister to another person through what Jesus Christ has done for me and to me" while "others have become brothers and sisters to me through what Jesus Christ has done for them and to them." Christ is central; Jesus is key to establishing the Christian community and uniting its members not only with himself but also to each other.

This makes the church a community unique from all other groups to which we belong. No other bonds of unity are stronger than those between Christ and each of us, and between persons united by faith in Christ. As Bonhoeffer says, "Our community consists solely in what Christ has done for both of us." Sisters and brothers are united around the deepest loyalty we know: Jesus Christ.

2 7

Equality of All in Christian Community

As the whole church now rests on the unity in Christ,
on the fact of "Christ existing as church-community,"
so all Christian community rests on the equality of all
established by God. (1:206–7)

╺╺╺

When we look around the church, throughout the world or in our own local congregations, we will notice the differences among people. Each one is unique. In the church community, differences may be striking: different cultures, races, personalities, and gifts. The list goes on.

But through all the differences—the "plurality"—is our "unity" (see 1 Corinthians 12:12-26). This is the unity of the body of Christ. As Bonhoeffer notes, this is the unity on which the church "rests." There is a unity of the Spirit in the church, a common bond of faith in Christ, a shared trust in God, and much more that unites us. We all have received salvation and forgiveness of sins in the cross of Jesus Christ.

Since Christ exists as the church community, Bonhoeffer concludes that "all Christian community rests on the equality of all established by God." All believers are equal in the sight of God. Bonhoeffer referred to Luther's doctrine of "the priesthood of all believers"—that all Christians can approach God through Jesus Christ and interpret Scripture in order to hear God's Word.

Someone has said there is only level ground at the foot of the cross. All believers receive the benefits of what Jesus Christ has done for our salvation. There are no "second class" Christians. The church is open to all, and in the church, there is a radical "equality of all" that is "established by God," said Bonhoeffer. The church sins when it creates distinctions among people and does not enact Christ's words of justice and peace for all people.

2 8

The Church as Gift and Task

We have to rediscover and revitalize the lost insight that all who are moved by the Spirit stand within the church, and that this is something that is both a gift [*Gabe*] and a task [*Aufgabe*]. (1:278)

⌐⌐⌐

When we think of the church, we realize that being part of the worldwide "communion of saints" who call Jesus Christ their Lord and Savior is a tremendous gift. We do not live our lives as Christians playing "solitaire." We are part of a worldwide fellowship of believers in Jesus Christ. We are also part of a local congregation where other believers, "ordinary people" in every way, do their best to be faithful disciples of Jesus Christ in a particular community. In the fellowship of the church, we are "priests to each other." We bear one another's burdens and are supported in the church community by others who carry us along through life. The church: what a gift!

Bonhoeffer affirms that "all who are moved by the Spirit stand within the church." We receive the gift of the church because we have received the gift of the Holy Spirit. The Spirit gives us faith to confess Jesus Christ. We become part of the church community and receive the wonderful gift of the church.

But Bonhoeffer goes on to note the church is "both a gift [*Gabe*] and a task [*Aufgabe*]." The German terms for "gift" and "task" are related. So Bonhoeffer means the gift of the church is received within the church's task, as the church carries out God's purposes. The church is a "task" in that it has a mission to carry out in this world. The church proclaims the gospel of Jesus Christ in word and deed. This is established in Jesus' parting words to his disciples: "Go therefore and make disciples of all nations" (Matthew 28:19). We are to proclaim Christ and make him known. This is our task.

The church: gift and task! Thank God for the church!

Christian Life

2 9

God's Path of Grace

Only one means of rescue remains, namely, God's path, and that means grace. But if it is by grace, it is no longer on the basis of works; otherwise grace would no longer be grace. But this means that the path to God is forever a hopeless one, if God does not come to us.... Not the path to God, but rather God's path to human beings, that is the sum total of Christianity. (10:483)

⇀⇀⇀

In a sermon in Barcelona on March 11, 1928, Bonhoeffer preached on a key emphasis of Martin Luther (1483–1546). His text was Romans 11:6: "But if it is by grace, it is no longer on the basis of works, otherwise grace would no longer be grace." Salvation is by God's grace.

There are two possible ways humans may receive salvation from God—the forgiveness of sins and reconciliation with our creator. One is to try to gain or merit God's favor by doing good works that are pleasing in God's sight. Perhaps if we do enough works, God will save us from our sin.

But Bonhoeffer proclaimed a different path. It is the path of God's grace. Bonhoeffer expounded his text that if salvation is by grace, "it is no longer on the basis of works;

otherwise grace would no longer be grace." Grace means God saves us out of God's love alone and not through any works we do.

If we cannot be saved by works we do, "the path to God is forever a hopeless one." Our only hope is that God comes to us: "Not the path to God, but rather God's path to human beings, that is the sum total of Christianity."

God comes to humanity in grace out of sheer love in Jesus Christ. Salvation is by God's grace alone!

3 0

The Trinity Dwells in Us

The incarnate, crucified, and transfigured one has entered into me and lives my life. "Christ is my life" (Philippians 1:21). But together with Christ, the Father also dwells in me; and both Father and Son dwell in me through the Holy Spirit. It is indeed the holy Trinity who dwells within Christians, who permeates them and changes them into the very image of the triune God. (4:287)

⸻

One of the great descriptions of the Christian life is when Paul said, "It is no longer I who live, but it is Christ who lives in me" (Galatians 2:20). By faith, Paul experienced a death to himself and a new life with Jesus Christ dwelling in him. As he also said, "For to me, living is Christ" (Philippians 1:21).

Bonhoeffer expanded on Paul's insight when he stressed that the Christ, who enters our life, is the one who was "incarnate, crucified, and transfigured." This is the Jesus we know from the Gospels. Jesus is the eternal Son of God who with the Holy Spirit and God the Father are the triune God we worship and adore: Father, Son, and Holy Spirit.

By the power of the Holy Spirit, Christ dwells in me, as does God the Father. In a breathtaking sentence, Bonhoeffer said that "it is indeed the holy Trinity who dwells within Christians." The eternal Trinity lives in us! The triune God "permeates" us and is with us in every dimension of who we are. The triune God "changes" us. God in us transforms us "into the very image of the triune God." Imagine that!

How important and exciting it is to realize that with our every breath, the holy Trinity is with us, working to enable us to live in the "image of the triune God"!

3 1

The Beyond in the Midst of Our Lives

God is the beyond in the midst of our lives. The church stands not at the point where human powers fail, at the boundaries, but in the center of the village. (8:367)

⌒⌒⌒

In prison, Bonhoeffer wrote of a "religionless Christianity." Contemporary people no longer saw religion as the beginning place when trying to understand themselves. What, then, were the basics of Christian faith in this "world come of age" when all that can endure is the core or heart of Christianity?

It seemed to Bonhoeffer that in the modern world, God is relegated to the background for the people of his time. God is perceived only as one who "waits in the wings" or exists only on the boundaries of life. A phrase Bonhoeffer used was *deus ex machina*—"god from the machine"—a term from the theater in ancient Greek and Roman times. A divine character "drops in" to the stage, supported by wires and pulleys ("machine") to resolve a conflict and save the day. Today, through science and technology, people can answer their own questions. They don't need a "god" to drop down and "save" them.

But Bonhoeffer argued that instead of God on the boundaries, "God is the beyond in the midst of our lives. The church stands not at the point where human powers fail, at the boundaries, but in the center of the village." God is there, in the center of our lives. In all we do, God is present. God has come to us in Jesus Christ, who shows us compassionate action in the world "for others." Christianity calls us to share God's sufferings in this world, in the sufferings of our neighbors, of all people. Experience God in Christ—in the midst of your life!

3 2

Assembling for Worship

Assembling for worship belongs to the essence of the
church-community. (1:230)

⌐⌐⌐

Theologically, the unity of the church is the work of God's
Spirit, uniting the body of Christ with Jesus Christ, the
"head of the church" (Ephesians 5:23). In the church's day-to-
day existence, it lives out this unity, in part, through assembling for worship. Bonhoeffer notes that "assembling for
worship belongs to the essence of the church-community."
Worship is central. Worship is the very nature of what it
means to be a church community and a Christian.

We cannot overstress the importance of the church
community's gathering for worship. The church gathers to
worship God in Jesus Christ. Bonhoeffer, as a Lutheran
Protestant, stressed that church assembles around the Word
of God. Worship, Bonhoeffer believed, consisted of the
preaching of the Word and the celebration of the sacraments.
Preaching is based on God's revelation in Scripture. The sacraments are visible expressions of God's Word. God's Word
and Spirit are at work as the assembly of the church community worships God.

In the assembly of the church community, God pledges to be present among the people, and the people pledge themselves to God as they experience God's Word to them. This assembly gives "visibility" to baptism, which imparts to us our identity in Christ. In the Lord's Supper, the church community proclaims the Lord's death to the world (1 Corinthians 11:26).

The people of Israel worshiped the God who pledged to be with them in covenant relationship. The people promised to be God's people and to serve the Lord. So the call goes out: "Make a joyful noise to the LORD, all the earth. Worship the LORD with gladness" (Psalm 100:1-2). Now the church community assembles to worship God in Jesus Christ, always with joy and gladness! Let us worship God!

3 3

Baptism Changes All Relationships

Baptism into the body of Christ changes not only a person's personal status with regard to salvation, but also their relationships throughout all of life. (4:235)

O ur baptism is a significant event. Whether we were baptized as infants or as adult believers in Jesus Christ, baptism incorporates us into the body of Christ, the church (Galatians 3:27-28). We are each baptized once into the community of salvation.

We do not offer baptism to God, but Jesus Christ offers baptism to us. In baptism, our lives are given to Christ as his possession. We become his "disciples." We are baptized "into Jesus Christ" (Romans 6:3; Matthew 28:19). Now we belong to Jesus. We belong to Jesus in the communal life of the church community.

Baptism makes all the difference in the world for us. Bonhoeffer wrote that "baptism into the body of Christ changes not only a person's personal status with regard to salvation, but also their relationships throughout all of life."

Baptism means our "break" with the world of living for ourselves. Baptism is death to "self" and receiving "new life" through Jesus Christ. Now we belong to Christ, and our relationship with the world is through Christ.

Baptism means forgiveness of sins. Our death in Christ by baptism means being freed from the power of sin because we are "baptized into his death" (Romans 6:3, 7). We die with Christ and rise with Christ into "newness of life" (6:4). We are "dead to sin and alive to God in Christ Jesus" (6:11).

In baptism we receive the Holy Spirit and are now able to "live by the Spirit" (Galatians 5:16). Our lives with others are marked by the "fruit of the Spirit" (Galatians 5:22-26). Now we are "burden-bearers" for others (Galatians 6:2).

Baptism changes all our relationships!

3 4

The Lord's Supper Is a Gift

The Lord's Supper is...a gift to the church-community.
Christ's presence in spirit is not merely symbolic, but a
given reality. Christ becomes alive in the believers as
church-community. (1:243)

⸺⸺⸺

The sacraments of the church are God's gifts to the church community. Bonhoeffer affirmed the key importance of baptism and the Lord's Supper as means of God's grace. In the sacraments, the Spirit of God is active in the believers who form a church congregation.

The nature of Christ's presence in the Lord's Supper was one of the most controversial issues of the sixteenth-century Protestant Reformations. Different streams of the Reformation—such as the Lutheran and the Reformed—disagreed on this issue. This, unfortunately, continued to divide Protestant groups.

Bonhoeffer affirmed the view of his Lutheran tradition that "Christ's presence in spirit is not merely symbolic, but a given reality." Christ is really present in the Supper. This is key for the sacrament to have power and blessing for those who eat the bread and drink the wine. The words of Jesus are significant: "This is my body" (1 Corinthians 11:24). For Bonhoeffer this meant Christ gives communion with himself in the Supper. Believers receive the body and blood of Christ. It also means that Christ renews the church congregation; according to Bonhoeffer, church members can be priests to each other—to bear each other's burdens (see Galatians 6:2) and to have their own burdens carried by others. This was emphasized by Luther and is called "the priesthood of all believers." It means a sharing of Christian love.

In short, said Bonhoeffer, "Christ becomes alive in the believers as church-community." This is the power of the Lord's Supper. The real presence of Christ unites believers with Christ and with one another. The Supper is a gift!

3 5

You Have Died and Been Raised

Christ came into the world not so that we should understand him but so that we should cling to him, so that we
simply let him pull us into the unbelievable event of the
resurrection, so that we simply have it said to us, said
to us in all its incomprehensibility: You have died—and
yet you have been raised! You are in the darkness—and
[yet] you are in the light. You are afraid—and yet you
can be glad. (11:464)

◡◡◡

For two Sundays in June 1932 (June 12 and 19), Bonhoeffer
preached on Colossians 3:1-4 at the Kaiser Wilhelm
Memorial Church in Berlin. He wanted to relate Paul's rich
text about the mystery of the Resurrection to the lives of this
congregation.

In the midst of social problems and personal problems
faced by everyone, Bonhoeffer affirms Paul's word that "you
have been raised with Christ" (Colossians 3:1), and "you have
died, and your life is hidden with Christ in God" (Colossians
3:3). These focus human life in the right place. Members of
the church community have not been left alone in lostness.
Jesus Christ has broken into the territory of death and lived

and died and been raised, pulling us up to God and defeating death.

This is the magnificent message of the gospel. Bonhoeffer said, "Christ came into the world not so that we should understand him but so that we should cling to him, so that we simply let him pull us into the unbelievable event of the resurrection." Resurrection is beyond our comprehension. But we cling to Christ and experience it! Now, "You have died—and yet you have been raised! You are in the darkness—and [yet] you are in the light. You are afraid—and yet you can be glad." Amen.

3 6

Good Works

We have been saved through God's own work in
Christ, rather than through our own works. Thus we
never derive any glory from our own works, for we ourselves are God's work. But this is why we have become
a new creation in Christ: to attain good works in him.
(4:278–79)

⇔⇔⇔⇔

Bonhoeffer is clear: Christian salvation rests on faith in
Jesus Christ. Only the work of Jesus Christ can bring salvation. Because of human sin, no one can do "good works"
to earn or deserve God's salvation. We cannot fulfill God's
law or merit God's good favor or justification. Only Jesus
Christ, through his death, can provide the way for salvation:
by faith in Jesus Christ (Romans 1:17).

Bonhoeffer affirmed that while we are saved by faith in
Jesus Christ, there is no true faith without the "good works"
that follow from faith. Faith in Jesus Christ propels us to do
works that are pleasing in God's sight, since they are God's
works in Christ. Paul wrote, "For we are what he has made
us, created in Christ Jesus for good works, which God pre-
pared beforehand to be our way of life" (Ephesians 2:10;

Colossians 1:10). If good works do not follow from faith, faith is not true or genuine.

God prepares good works for us. So, says Bonhoeffer, "we never derive any glory from our own works, for we ourselves are God's work." Our good works are to be unconscious, even "unknown" to believers (Matthew 6:3). The righteous at the last judgment will be surprised: "Lord, when was it?" (Matthew 25:37). "But," says Bonhoeffer, "this is why we have become a new creation in Christ: to attain good works in him." We are saved by "faith alone," but not a "faith that is alone"—good works follow faith.

3 7

Drawing Breath from God

Prayer is drawing breath from God; prayer means surrendering and consecrating one's life to God; prayer means confiding in God. (10:555)

~~~

People think of prayer in different ways.

For some, prayer is primarily what we do in church. We may listen to prayers or participate in prayers. Personally, perhaps we pray on occasion when we have a meal or go to bed at night. Or when we have a particular problem or face a difficulty, we may pray to God.

Bonhoeffer wanted Christians to realize prayer is much more vital and important than being only an occasional practice. Prayer is essential for our lives as well as our faith. Bonhoeffer said, "Prayer is drawing breath from God; prayer means surrendering and consecrating one's life to God; prayer means confiding in God."

This puts prayer at the very basis of life itself—"drawing breath from God." We read in Genesis 2:7 that God breathed into the first human "the breath of life," which brought life. Now too we continue to draw breath from God. We depend on our creator and loving Lord for every breath we take!

Prayer means "surrendering and consecrating one's life to God," said Bonhoeffer. The life we have from God, we give back to God by living in relationship with God and following God's will and way for us. We find this will and way as disciples of Jesus Christ.

Prayer also means "confiding in God." That is, with every breath, we can recognize God's presence and express all things to God. Paul said, "Let your requests be made known to God" (Philippians 4:6). We can let our requests, our sins, our thanksgiving and gratitude—all that is important to us— be made known to God. We can confide in God in all things!

3 8

New Every Morning

Just as the ancient sun rises daily anew, so also is God's eternal mercy new every morning (Lamentations 3:23). Being able to grasp God's ancient faithfulness anew each morning, being able to begin a new life with God daily in the midst of one's present life with God, that is the gift God gives us with each new morning. (14:864)

❧❧❧

Morning is an important time. It begins our new day. It marks a safe passage through the night when in sleep and helplessness, we commend ourselves to God's care.

In the morning, we again commend ourselves to God's care as we face a new day. Bonhoeffer reminds us that "just as the ancient sun rises daily anew," so we begin life anew in the morning. As we do, we remember that "God's eternal mercy" is "new every morning" as well. He echoes the book of Lamentations: "The steadfast love of the LORD never ceases, his mercies never come to an end; they are new every morning; great is your faithfulness" (Lamentations 3:22-23).

God's presence with us and care for us, in God's eternal mercy, is God's blessed gift to us. That mercy is eternal, but it is also new every morning. It is sure because God is faithful.

Great is God's faithfulness to us! We receive the gift of life each day from the God who preserves our lives. We receive God's love and grace because God keeps faith with us who are God's covenant people. Each morning is new as our lives become new, being lived in the midst of the presence of God.

God's faithfulness to us is nothing less than God's grace. God's grace is the gift God gives us each morning. Let us begin each day grateful for God's faithful mercy and the gift of life God gives!

3 9

Jesus Lives in Believers

The life of Jesus Christ here on earth has not yet concluded. Christ continues to live it in the lives of his followers. (4:286)

⇀⇀⇀

Those who have been justified by faith and live as God's church community through the power of the Holy Spirit (sanctification) experience Jesus living in the lives of believers. Jesus Christ indwells our hearts. We live life with Christ, which is a "crucified life" (Galatians 2:19), a life that follows Christ into suffering and follows him where he leads. In death and resurrection, believers are transformed into the image of the risen Christ, "seeing the glory of the Lord" (2 Corinthians 3:18).

In a real sense, according to Bonhoeffer, "the life of Jesus Christ here on earth has not yet concluded. Christ continues to live it in the lives of his followers." This is what discipleship is all about: following Jesus. Paul said, "I have been crucified with Christ; and it is no longer I who live, but it is Christ who lives in me" (Galatians 2:19-20). Christ lives in the church community and in the lives of his disciples. As Paul put it, succinctly, "To me, living is Christ" (Philippians 1:21).

For us, it is good to realize that we continue the life of Christ in the lives we live in faith. The church community is the corporate expression of Jesus Christ, who lived, was crucified, and raised again by the power of God. The church is the ongoing way that Jesus' ministry continues to be expressed in this world. All believers have ministries of Christ to carry out, continuations of the ministries begun by Jesus during his days on earth.

Our blessing and responsibility as we "know Christ" is to "make him known" in our words and deeds. Christ continues to live in us!

4 0

Jesus' Word Speaks to Us

There is no age, no moment in life when Jesus's word
does not have something to say to us. (10:493)

⌐⌐⌐

When Bonhoeffer preached in Barcelona, Spain, on April
15, 1928, on the first Sunday after Easter, he told the
congregation that the resurrected Christ is always with us.
Jesus is with us through his will and through his word. Jesus'
word expresses his will. When we read and hear Jesus' word,
we sense Christ's presence.

Jesus' word is always the same, yet always different. Jesus'
word always tells us of God's love for us; that God calls us
to love and serve God and others; that God leads and guides
our lives.

Yet, in every moment, Jesus' word speaks to us in new
and fresh ways. Jesus' word means something different to different people; it means something different to us at various
points in our lives. But Bonhoeffer declared, "There is no age,
no moment in life when Jesus's word does not have something
to say to us." Our whole lives are affected by Jesus' word.
In every time and place and situation, Jesus is speaking to
us. He makes his will known to us. He helps us know what

to believe, what directions to take, what decisions to make. Jesus' word speaks during our whole lives.

Through all Jesus says is the Easter promise of the resurrected Christ: "I am with you always" (Matthew 28:20). As we hear Jesus' word in Scripture, in the preached Word and sacraments, and through the fellowship of the church community, we experience Jesus' presence. We meet him in our lonely hours and in our joys. We encounter Christ in the people we meet. We find Christ in blessings we receive. Speak, Lord Jesus!

4 1

The Temptation of Jesus in Us

The faithful must learn to understand all their temptations as the temptation of Jesus Christ in them, and
thus they will partake of his overcoming. (15:402)

———

After his baptism by John the Baptist, Jesus was "tempted
by the devil" in the wilderness (Matthew 4:1-11). Jesus
was tested to see if he would turn aside from his mission and
allow himself to be drawn into the lures of evil. If he yielded,
he would be unfaithful to God and could not accomplish
God's will. But Jesus did not give in to the devil. He resisted
and remained faithful to God.

Temptation is real for us as Christians today. We too face
testings. We have the urge to give in to the powers of evil and
follow that path instead of the way of Jesus.

Bonhoeffer maintained that "the faithful must learn to
understand all their temptations as the temptation of Jesus
Christ in them, and thus they will partake of his overcoming." Bonhoeffer urges us that when tempted, we must realize
temptation has been overcome by Jesus, who has acted in our
place. He has overcome the power of temptation that calls
us to turn away from God's will for us. Our temptations are

temptations Jesus faced...and conquered. His victory is our victory.

In a real sense, Jesus is tempted in us. We can claim his power and his conquest as our own. Jesus has acted for us. When tempted, we say to God: Look at the temptation of Jesus Christ your Son; and "lead us not into temptation" (Matthew 6:13). We enter into Jesus' temptations, and Jesus enters into our temptations. As we participate in his temptations, we also participate in the victories Jesus has won.

This is a great blessing. Jesus helps us in our temptations by conquering temptations for us!

4 2

Christ Shows Us What to Do

From Christ alone we must know what we should do.
Not, however, from him as the preaching prophet of
the Sermon on the Mount, but rather from him who
gives us life and forgiveness, as the one who has fulfilled God's commandments for us, as the one who
brings and promises the new world. (11:363)

⁓⁓⁓

In a sense, our view of the future pulls us forward in life.
We often think it is the past that shapes us. It does, to a
certain extent. But our view of the future gets us out of bed
in the morning. We face a new day because we believe it is
worth it, that our lives are moving along to a future that is
drawing us into what it has in store.

What we do along the way to the future is our question.
Disciples of Jesus Christ set what we do in relation to what
Jesus says and the directions he points us. Discipleship, as
Bonhoeffer emphasized, is "following Jesus." In a 1932
address to an international youth conference, Bonhoeffer
said, "From Christ alone we must know what we should do."

But Bonhoeffer went on to indicate that while Christ
instructs us as a "preaching prophet of the Sermon on the

Mount," there is another reason we follow his word to us: "Christ is the one who gives us life and forgiveness, as the one who has fulfilled God's commandments for us, as the one who brings and promises the new world." Jesus brought and promised a coming kingdom of God—a new world where God's reign is fully realized (Luke 13:29).

God's reign pulls us forward in life. It gives us purpose and meaning. We have new life and forgiveness in Christ. We follow Jesus!

4 3

All Prayers Are Answered in Christ

We may be certain that our prayer will be heard because
it issues from God's Word and promise. Because God's
Word has found its fulfillment in Jesus Christ, all the
prayers we pray on the basis of this Word are certainly
fulfilled and answered in Jesus Christ. (5:89)

B onhoeffer advocated that our prayers be made on the
basis of Scripture. He believed the words of the Bible
should guide our prayers. He wanted Christians to let the
Scriptures speak to our conditions and needs. In light of the
Scriptures, we can ask God for God's guidance and help.
For example, the Lord's Prayer offers directions for our own
prayers (Matthew 6:7-15).

When our prayers emerge from engaging God's Word in
Scripture, we have assurance our prayers will be answered.
God promises to hear our prayers and answer them.
Bonhoeffer put it this way: "Because God's Word has found
its fulfillment in Jesus Christ, all the prayers we pray on the
basis of this Word are certainly fulfilled and answered in
Jesus Christ."

It is helpful to heed Bonhoeffer's direction here and let our prayers emerge in relation to our reading of Scripture. Our various kinds of prayers—such as prayers of praise and adoration, confession, thanksgiving, and supplication or intercession as we pray for others—all have their roots in Scripture. Our prayers can gain focus when they rise from the Bible.

Prayers made on the basis of the Word ground our prayers in God's will as we understand God's will through reading the Bible. In Scripture reading, we also seek the guidance of the Holy Spirit to enlighten our minds and speak to our hearts. Then our prayers are offered to God in the deep assurance that God hears and answers. Pray, and keep praying!

4 4

God in the Midst of Anguish

The joy of God has gone through the poverty of the
manger and the agony of the cross; that is why it is
invincible, irrefutable. It does not deny the anguish,
when it is there, but finds God in the midst of it, in
fact precisely there; it does not deny grave sin but finds
forgiveness precisely in this way; it looks death straight
in the eye, but it finds life precisely within it. (16:378)

B onhoeffer sent a circular letter to those who were students at the Finkenwalde seminary, which was established as an alternative to the theological education offered
by the German state church.

His Advent 1942 letter acknowledged those who had
died—many in the war—since the last letter. These deaths
were a sadness, helped only by the joy of God. True joy,
Bonhoeffer recognized, comes from God. It is not a "joy"
that overlooks the agony and anguish of the human heart.
The psalmist acknowledged, "I suffered distress and anguish"
(Psalm 116:3-4).

God has met anguish head-on as well. Our joy in the midst

of anguish has to come from God and is God. Bonhoeffer wrote,

> The joy of God has gone through the poverty of the manger and the agony of the cross; that is why it is invincible, irrefutable. It does not deny the anguish, when it is there, but finds God in the midst of it, in fact precisely there; it does not deny grave sin but finds forgiveness precisely in this way; it looks death straight in the eye, but it finds life precisely within it.

God is found in the midst of anguish because God has gone through the anguishes of our lives, even suffering and death in Jesus Christ. Now we can find life within death. God is with us!

4 5

God's Gifts—Our Responsibility

If we want to understand God's loving-kindness in
God's gifts to us, we must see them as responsibility
for our brother. No one should say: God has blessed
me with money and possessions, and then live now as
if he and his loving God were alone in the world. Then
the hour will come when he [must] see that he has wor-
shipped the false god of his own happiness and selfishness. The blessing and the loving-kindness of God are
not possessions but responsibility. (11:405)

⟶⟶⟶

A strong Old Testament term is the Hebrew *ḥesed*. This
word is often translated in the King James Version as
"lovingkindness." In other translations it is "steadfast love."

In a sermon on Psalm 63:3 on October 4, 1931, Bonhoeffer
spoke about God's "lovingkindness" expressed in God's gifts
to us. These gifts must be seen as bringing responsibility for
others. Our blessings are not ours to deserve or hoard. Today,
some speak of a "prosperity gospel" in which God blesses
us because of our actions, so we deserve the prosperity we
receive. This is wrong. Nor are God's blessings given to provide a cozy personal relationship with God, as if only God

and I exist in the world. These attitudes will lead to the realization that we have worshiped the "false god" of our "own happiness and selfishness."

God's steadfast love is greater than even our blessings. For God's "steadfast love is better than life" (Psalm 63:3). It is *hesed* that counts. Our blessings from God are not the "ultimates." God is ultimate. God's love is better than life itself. Our blessings and "the loving-kindness of God are not possessions but responsibility." God's gifts lead us to bless others. God blessed Abram "so that you will be a blessing" (Genesis 12:2). Are we?

4 6

Blessing the World

Blessing means laying one's hand on something and saying: Despite everything, you belong to God. This is what we do with the world that inflicts such suffering on us. We do not abandon it; we do not repudiate, despise, or condemn it. Instead we call it back to God, we give it hope, we lay our hand on it and say: may God's blessing come upon you, may God renew you; be blessed, world created by God, you who belong to your Creator and Redeemer. (16:632)

⚊⚊⚊

In June 1944, Bonhoeffer was in Tegel prison. There he wrote a meditation on the daily texts for June 8, 1944, which he sent to his friend Eberhard Bethge. One of the texts was 1 Peter 3:9: "Do not repay evil for evil or abuse for abuse; but, on the contrary, repay with a blessing."

Bonhoeffer noted that it is the righteous who suffer from unrighteousness in this world. When righteous persons bring God's perspective into the world, they suffer as God suffers in the world. But God's help is always present. In suffering, the righteous find God. God is their help.

The righteous respond to their suffering...by blessing. This was God's response to the world that crucified Jesus Christ—blessing. Without blessing, there is no hope.

The world lives by God's blessing. In our quotation, Bonhoeffer says that in our suffering, we should not despise or condemn the world; we should call it back to God. We "bless," which means "laying one's hand on something and saying: Despite everything, you belong to God." We give hope to the world. We say: "May God's blessing come upon you, may God renew you; be blessed, world created by God, you who belong to your Creator and Redeemer."

In our sufferings, we say: "Be blessed."

4 7

Filled to the Brim with God's Goodness

> I am so certain of God's hand and guidance that I hope
> I may be kept in such certainty always. You must never
> doubt that I am thankfully and cheerfully going along
> the path on which I am being led. My past life is filled
> to the brim with God's goodness, and the forgiving love
> of the Crucified covers my guilt. (8:517)

‿‿‿

Within a year of writing to Eberhard Bethge on August 23, 1944, Dietrich Bonhoeffer was dead. His letters from prison expressed his life of faith as he edged toward his death.

Bonhoeffer urged his friend not to have anxious thoughts or worry about him in prison. Bonhoeffer wanted Bethge to remember to pray for him, knowing for certain Bethge would not forget this. Then, Bonhoeffer wrote,

> I am so certain of God's hand and guidance that I hope
> I may be kept in such certainty always. You must never
> doubt that I am thankfully and cheerfully going along
> the path on which I am being led. My past life is filled to

the brim with God's goodness, and the forgiving love of
the Crucified covers my guilt.

Through the zigs and zags of his life, Bonhoeffer was sure
of God's guiding, providential hand. This was a certainty
Bonhoeffer wished to maintain as he proceeded "along the
path on which I am being led."

Here, Bonhoeffer expressed two of the most important
things we can experience: our past life being "filled to the
brim with God's goodness"—as the psalmist said, we are
"satisfied with good" as long as we live (Psalm 103:5). We
also have our guilt covered by "the forgiving love of the
Crucified" (1 John 1:7). God's goodness fills us through our
years. Christ lovingly forgives us and cleanses us!

Part 2

Living as a Christian

Following Jesus

4 8

Discipleship Is Joy

Where will the call to discipleship lead those who follow it? What decisions and painful separations will it
entail? We must take this question to him who alone
knows the answer. Only Jesus Christ, who bids us follow him, knows where the path will lead. But we know
that it will be a path full of mercy beyond measure.
Discipleship is joy. (4:40)

⌐⌐⌐

To be a disciple of Jesus Christ means to follow Jesus.
This was Jesus' call to his first followers: "If any want to
become my followers, let them deny themselves and take up
their cross and follow me" (Mark 8:34).

Bonhoeffer's book *Discipleship* was published in 1937
and was first titled in English as *The Cost of Discipleship*.
The current title, *Discipleship*, captures the German title,
Nachfolge, which literally means "following after." To be a
disciple of Jesus Christ means to "follow after" Jesus.

Bonhoeffer's whole life and theology can nearly be
summed up in this basic idea of discipleship as "following
after" Christ. He did not know—nor do we—where the call
to discipleship may lead. There will be difficult decisions that

can bring painful separations. Jesus implied this when he said his disciples were to "take up their cross and follow." Only Jesus, says Bonhoeffer, knows where the path of discipleship will lead. Our focus is on Jesus, and we do not know in what directions following will take us.

But Bonhoeffer believed one thing was certain: our paths will be paths of mercy "beyond measure." Through it all, "discipleship is joy."

Following Jesus brings us the deepest joy we can know in life. He leads us into the unknown, but he is always with us. He is our companion. We follow him. Jesus brings us joy we can never imagine!

4 9

Jesus Calls Us to Life

"Faith" is something whole and involves one's whole life. Jesus calls not to a new religion but to life. (8:482)

⇀⇀⇀

In Christian faith, it is always a temptation to look on our actions and activities as means to turn us into certain kinds of people. We participate in various religious practices thinking they can make us into people who will be acceptable in the sight of God. We may go through the same rituals week after week: attend Sunday school and church, and perhaps another service through the week. We do certain things every day to show we are the kind of person God should accept and bless.

We should hope to be delivered from these kinds of attitudes. We know they are not the essence of true Christian faith. If we listen to Jesus, we hear him saying, "I came that they may have life, and have it abundantly" (John 10:10). Jesus came to bring us "life," not a form of "religion" that squeezes us into its mold. We are not saved by our religious practices. We are saved by faith in Jesus Christ, who brings us an abundant life that frees us to serve Christ by serving others in the world.

Bonhoeffer put it clearly when he wrote that " 'Faith' is something whole and involves one's whole life. Jesus calls not to a new religion but to life." True faith is the faith that expresses itself in discipleship, in following Jesus. It is the total commitment of one's total life to loving and serving Jesus Christ. This is true life, the "abundant life" Jesus brings. This is the free life in Christ's service. We do not seek to justify ourselves or make ourselves acceptable to God. We receive the abundant life Christ brings!

5 0

Self-Denial

Self-denial means knowing only Christ, no longer knowing oneself. It means no longer seeing oneself, only him who is going ahead, no longer seeing the way which is too difficult for us. Self-denial says only: he is going ahead; hold fast to him. (4:86)

⌐⌐⌐

There is a radical nature to Christian discipleship, to following Jesus Christ. Discipleship is radical because it affects us at our "roots," the depth of our beings. If we follow Jesus, we must give up all things—including our selves—to be Jesus' disciples and move through life in the direction Jesus points us.

Bonhoeffer points us to the core of discipleship, which is self-denial. He wrote, "Self-denial means knowing only Christ, no longer knowing oneself. It means no longer seeing oneself, only him who is going ahead, no longer seeing the way which is too difficult for us. Self-denial says only: he is going ahead; hold fast to him."

Our single-minded devotion in following Jesus is to say no to ourselves and yes to Jesus. This is what our Master meant when he said, "If any want to become my followers, let them deny themselves and take up their cross and follow me" (Matthew 16:24). Self-denial is the essential condition for discipleship. Self-denial is at the heart of what it means to be a Christian. We know Jesus Christ, and he is the one we follow, not ourselves.

In this discipleship, we do not seek our own ways through life. We look to Jesus, the one who is "going ahead." We follow after Christ. We seek only his way to be our way. We trust Jesus, even when our way is unknown or unclear or seemingly too hard for us to follow.

Very simply: Jesus is going ahead. We "hold fast" to him!

5 1

Cheap Grace

Cheap grace is preaching forgiveness without repentance; it is baptism without the discipline of community; it is the Lord's Supper without confession of sin; it is absolution without personal confession. Cheap grace is grace without discipleship, grace without the cross, grace without the living, incarnate Jesus Christ. (4:44)

━━━

Bonhoeffer began his book *Discipleship* (formerly called *The Cost of Discipleship*) by talking about "cheap grace." In essence, this is the "grace" Christians want, but they want to receive it without cost to themselves. It is an easy Christianity in which there are no demands for a life that is different from the life the "world" lives, and there is no need to follow Jesus Christ. As Bonhoeffer put it,

Cheap grace is preaching forgiveness without repentance; it is baptism without the discipline of community; it is the Lord's Supper without confession of sin; it is absolution without personal confession. Cheap grace is grace without discipleship, grace without the cross, grace without the living, incarnate Jesus Christ.

Bonhoeffer's book contrasted "cheap grace" with "costly grace," which is the life of Christian discipleship. Cheap grace is easy for us to desire. It is the attractive hope that we can receive God's gracious benefits without having our lives affected by the challenges and demands of the Christian gospel Bonhoeffer described. We want to live safe and secure lives, possessing a grace that takes care of everything so we do not have to repent or sacrifice or give up ourselves in order to follow Jesus. This is a grace that is self-sufficient, with no need for participation in a Christian community of faith. It is grace without a cross, said Bonhoeffer, and is truly "grace without the living, incarnate Jesus Christ." The rich ruler could not sacrifice to follow Jesus (Luke 18:18-25). He wanted cheap grace. Do we?

5 2

Costly Grace

> Costly grace...is the costly pearl, for whose price the
> merchant sells all that he has....It is the call of Jesus
> Christ which causes a disciple to leave his nets and fol-
> low him....It is costly, because it calls to discipleship;
> it is grace, because it calls us to follow *Jesus Christ.*
> ...Above all, it is grace because the life of God's Son
> was not too costly for God to give in order to make us
> live. God did, indeed, give him up for us. Costly grace
> is the incarnation of God. (4:44–45)

⇁⇁⇁

Costly grace is the incarnation of God." Costly grace
is Jesus Christ. For Bonhoeffer this is the grace of
Christian discipleship, which defines what it means to be a
Christian. This is the grace we, like the merchant in Jesus'
parable, find as "one pearl of great value," which means
so much that the merchant "sold all he had and bought it"
(Matthew 13:45-46).

Costly grace is the call of Jesus Christ to which we, like
his first disciples, leave all to follow him (Mark 1:16-20). This
grace costs us our life—the life we naturally want to live for
ourselves. Now, we live for Jesus Christ. But this costly grace

is "grace" because by giving up ourselves, we are able to live the true life God intends. This is by God's grace, by the love of God who sent Jesus Christ to live and die for us sinful people.

There is no cost too great for us to give—even ourselves. There was no cost too great for God to give—God gave the life of God's Son so we can live. We were bought by this price (1 Corinthians 6:20). We give back to God the lives we owe God—by following Jesus Christ. "Costly grace!"

5 3

Jesus Abides with Us

Jesus is the Lord of the ages and is always with his own, even when things are difficult, and will abide with us; that is our comfort. If tribulation and anxiety come upon us, Jesus is with us and leads us over into God's eternal kingdom. (10:495)

⟶⟶⟶

There are times we need to hear and receive the great truths of the Christian faith that affirm God's everlasting presence and power: "From everlasting to everlasting you are God" (Psalm 90:2). "Do not be afraid; I am the first and the last" (Revelation 1:17; cf. Isaiah 41:4); "Jesus Christ is the same yesterday and today and forever" (Hebrews 13:8). These wonderful words of Scripture sustain us, assuring us of God's greatness and presence in the world.

At times we need to hear and receive these promises on a very personal level. When tragedy strikes, when difficulties arise, when we feel a power failure of the Spirit, we need to know the promises in the words of Scripture also have a personal dimension. They are for me.

In a 1928 sermon in Barcelona, Bonhoeffer assured the congregation that Jesus Christ is God with us, always. He could have quoted Jesus' promise to his disciples: "Abide in me as I abide in you" (John 15:4). Bonhoeffer proclaimed, "Jesus is the Lord of the ages and is always with his own, even when things are difficult, and will abide with us; that is our comfort. If tribulation and anxiety come upon us, Jesus is with us and leads us over into God's eternal kingdom."

Jesus abides with us and in us, when all else fails and days are darkest. This is our greatest comfort and hope. Now and forever, Jesus abides with us. Make that promise your own, today: "I abide in you."

5 4

Be Like Christ

The content of the Christian message...is that we should be like Christ himself. No method leads to this end, only faith. (6:150)

⸺⸺⸺

Discipleship, or following Jesus, was a key emphasis for Bonhoeffer. The follower of Jesus commits oneself fully, without reserve, to living in the direction Jesus points. We move into that path in obedience to Jesus who says, "Follow me" (Mark 2:14).

As disciples, we follow Jesus into the world. Our model for discipleship, our norm for living, is Jesus himself. We do not need rules or regulations to show us our way as much as a living example of how God wants us to live. We find this in Jesus himself. Jesus is our example, the one who points our way.

Bonhoeffer put this succinctly when he wrote, "The content of the Christian message...is that we should be like Christ himself. No method leads to this end, only faith." We do not seek guidance or a "how to" book to instruct us in Christian discipleship. We follow Jesus, and in following we seek to "be like Christ himself." This is "the content of the

Christian message," said Bonhoeffer, and it identifies us as Christ's disciples.

"Be like Christ." That is easily said but harder to do. Bonhoeffer spoke of true discipleship as "costly grace." This grace costs us our whole life: self-denial. We give up ourselves to follow one greater than ourselves, one who calls us to complete obedience and service.

When we are being like Christ, we give up ourselves for the sake of others. This is what Jesus did. Sometimes this leads to unpopular or dangerous actions. Our radical obedience to Jesus leads us to radical self-giving to those who suffer, those in need. Jesus gave up himself "for others." So do we!

55

Who Is Christ for Us Today?

What keeps gnawing at me is the question, what is Christianity, or who is Christ actually for us today. …We are approaching a completely religionless age; people as they are now simply cannot be religious anymore. (8:362)

—→—

Bonhoeffer's *Letters and Papers from Prison* provides us with his thoughts at the end of his life in the months prior to his execution. These "theological letters," many written to Bonhoeffer's friend Eberhard Bethge, have become a classic work. They show Bonhoeffer, connected with the plot to assassinate Hitler, as a person of faith and prayer, deeply reflecting on Christian faith and what it means to be a Christian in the modern world.

Bonhoeffer's focus on the world is captured in the question from our quotation: "Who is Christ actually for us today?" It is not enough to know only what the church has historically said about "who" Jesus is. We must understand what it means that we confess Jesus Christ today, now!

Bonhoeffer's phrase "religionless age" is associated with his term "religionless Christianity." He is pointing toward people in the secular world who live as though there is no "God." This is a "world come of age." People do not feel they need to look to "God."

But Bonhoeffer was convinced this situation means God is not just an "idea." God is to be found as a living reality in the center of life—in the core of the gospel: Jesus died on the cross. Jesus is at the center of life. Jesus is with us and helps us. We find God in Jesus Christ today as the one who helps us in his weakness and suffering (2 Corinthians 13:4).

Disciples of Jesus Christ will live the way of Christ. We live a "secular life" in the midst of the world, not withdrawn. We follow Jesus in faith, taking responsibility for others and loving them because God has loved us, utterly, in Jesus Christ.

5 6

Jesus Encounters Us

Jesus Christ is not only with us in lonely hours; Jesus
Christ also encounters us in every step we take, in every
person we meet. (10:494)

━ ━ ━

On the first Sunday after Easter, April 15, 1928,
Bonhoeffer preached at a Lutheran church in Barcelona,
Spain, where he was serving as a pastoral assistant (German:
Vikar).

Bonhoeffer's sermon may be titled "God Is with Us." Here
he mentioned ancient fairy tales and legends of God walking
among human beings. But sin occurred, and there was a rift
between God and humans. This "eternal distance" showed
when "humanity raised its hand against the God dwelling
among them and nailed Jesus Christ to the cross—Good
Friday." But on Easter, Jesus was raised from the dead. Now,
"I am with you [Matthew 28:20]...that is the Easter message, not the distant, but the nearby God, that is Easter."

Bonhoeffer said, "the only important thing" is "to keep
our eyes open to see where we find God." God is with us, in
Jesus. He is "not only with us in lonely hours; Jesus Christ
also encounters us in every step we take, in every person we

meet." God now speaks to us "from every human being; the other person." This person is God's claim on us. Bonhoeffer told his congregation, "God's claim is made on us in the wanderer on the street, the beggar at the door, the sick person at the door of the church, though certainly no less in every person near to us, in every person with whom we are together daily." This energizes our human relationships because in the "other," we receive God's appeal to us. In the other, we see the face of Jesus. Jesus encounters us in "one of the least of these" (Matthew 25:45)—and in all persons.

5 7

The Church of Faith, Not Success

In the world it is important to be able to point to the
great things one has done, but the church that did that
would be showing that it has become enslaved to the
laws and the powers of this world. *The church of success* is truly far from being *the church of faith.* (13:393)

⌒⌒⌒

No doubt we live in a culture that honors and propels us
toward "success." What "success" is varies for each of
us. But drives for wealth, power, celebrity, and happiness are
part of a "cult of success" for many people.

Bonhoeffer told his London congregation that while "in
the world it is important to be able to point to the great things
one has done," it is not the same for the church. If the church
adopted the standards of the world for "success"—proclaiming what great things it has done—"it would be showing that
it has become enslaved to the laws and the powers of this
world." This is a great temptation: to think the church—like
other institutions or like our own lives—should seek some
kind of "success" that will be recognized like the world rec-
ognizes "success" in other aspects of society.

But giving into this temptation of seeking "success" like this shows the "laws and powers of the world" have captured a church. "Success" is not a biblical category. God does not call the church to be "successful." God calls the church to be "faithful." As Bonhoeffer put it, "The church of success is truly far from being the church of faith."

Was Jesus "successful"? In this same sermon on 1 Corinthians 13:13, Bonhoeffer said the cross of Golgotha is what God's "success" looks like. In the church, we live by faith, not "success" as the world sees it!

5 8

Death Fulfills Our Life with Christ

> Those who live with Christ die daily to their own will.
> Christ in us gives us over to death so that he can live
> within us. Thus our inner dying grows to meet that
> death from without. Christians receive their own death
> in this way, and in this way our physical death very
> truly becomes not the end but rather the fulfillment of
> our life with Jesus Christ. Here we enter into commu-
> nity with the One who at his own death was able to say,
> "It is finished" [John 19:30]. (16:208)

The Christian life is a daily dying to one's self. We die
daily to our own will and follow the will of God in Jesus
Christ. Our self-death enables Christ to live in us. This is
basic to Christian discipleship, as Bonhoeffer often made
clear.

As we die daily, we move toward our own physical death.
In this way, our inner death meets our outer death. This
means, said Bonhoeffer, that "our physical death very truly
becomes not the end but rather the fulfillment of our life
with Jesus Christ. Here we enter into community with the

One who at his own death was able to say, 'It is finished' [John 19:30]."

At our physical death, we are joined perfectly with Christ into the fullness of community. Our physical death is the end of our life's outward journey. But it is more truly the "fulfillment of our life with Jesus Christ." In death we can come into an eternal unity or community with Christ. This is the end toward which we have moved throughout all our years. We will be united with Christ in the fullness of life, which the Scriptures call "eternal life." Jesus' word "It is finished" (John 19:30) is our word too!

Living Before God

5 9

God's Interruptions

> We must be ready to allow ourselves to be interrupted
> by God, who will thwart our plans and frustrate our
> ways time and again, even daily, by sending people
> across our path with their demands and requests. (5:99)

⌐⌐⌐

It is easy to live our days intent on our own agendas. We
have things we must get done. We have limited time. We
move through our "to do" lists so we don't get behind and
can follow our plans to their completion.

But what about when interruptions occur? There are
things that slow us down from doing what we need to get
done. These intrusions break up the day and threaten to put
us behind on our checklists of things to do.

We often resent the interruptions because they threaten to
thwart our plans. But Bonhoeffer raises the question of what
if people are sent by God to cross our paths "with demands
and requests"—like the situation the Samaritan encountered
with the man who was beaten by robbers in Jesus' parable
(Luke 10:25-37). What was the Samaritan to do? What do
we do? Will we turn away? Will we grudgingly help others
with their problems? What will our attitudes be?

Bonhoeffer tells us we must be ready "to allow ourselves to be interrupted by God" through these other people who need us. God is showing us what really matters. It is not the accomplishment of our agendas. What counts most is being attentive to God's work and our parts in it by meeting needs. Our attitudes are important here. If we are too busy to be interrupted by God, we are too busy. We are missing the sign of the cross in our lives, absolutizing our own desires and plans. Be ready to experience divine interruptions to follow God's way.

6 0

Pay Attention to the Word Alone

We should pay attention to the Word alone and leave it
to the Word to deal effectively with everything. (5:88)

⇁⇁⇁

We are bombarded on every side by information, suggestions, commands, and words to shape our minds and hearts. Wherever we turn, these words keep coming to us.

In the midst, we need to stop. We need to be quiet and meditate. We need to meditate on God's Word, paying attention to God's Word alone, as Bonhoeffer says.

God's Word should be our focus as Christian people. We listen to what God says to us. Sometimes God's Word is hard to hear. Bonhoeffer noted there are hours of "emptiness and dryness." We live through these times, so we might "once again expect everything from God's Word." In times of emptiness, we long and yearn for God's Word. As God said to the psalmist, "Incline your ears to the words of my mouth" (Psalm 78:1). When we do this—and when we hear God's Word—we have the freedom to "leave it to the Word to deal effectively with everything," said Bonhoeffer. We pay attention to God's Word and trust God's Word.

Bonhoeffer believed a result is that we will "gain happiness." He quoted the spiritual writer Thomas à Kempis, who said, "Seek God, not happiness." This is our basic rule in meditation. For Bonhoeffer, "If you seek God alone, you will gain happiness." This is "the promise of all meditation."

True happiness in life comes from living before God and paying attention to God's Word. God's Word enables us to deal with all we have to face in life. When we incline our ears to God's Word, we trust God. In meditation we find we receive all things through the God who speaks to us.

6 1

Think of Yourself in the Right Way

"Do not claim to be wiser than you are" (Romans
12:17 [Romans 12:16b NRSV]). Only those who live
by the forgiveness of their sin in Jesus Christ will think
of themselves in the right way. (5:96)

━━━

When Bonhoeffer discussed service in *Life Together*,
he turned to Romans 12, which provides important
insights. Those who have received God's mercy in Jesus
Christ will want to serve others. They serve not from posi-
tions of judgment—they do not believe they are "better" than
others and should exercise power over them. Nor do they
serve from a desire to gain fame or notoriety or "celebrity."
Paul instructed the Roman Christians "not to think of yourself more highly than you ought to think" (Romans 12:3).
Knowing who we truly are—sinners saved by God's grace in
Jesus Christ (Ephesians 2:8)—is the basis for our service in
Christ to others. Paul says, "Do not be haughty, but associate
with the lowly" (Romans 12:16).

Our true knowledge of ourselves in relation to God in
Christ means no one should "claim to be wiser than you are"
(Romans 12:16b). For, as Bonhoeffer wrote, "only those who

live by the forgiveness of their sin in Jesus Christ will think of themselves in the right way." The right knowledge of ourselves means we know our own "self-wisdom" comes to an end when we are forgiven by Christ. We are humble. Our own plans and intentions will always be subject to Christ's will. We will put the will of our neighbors in front of our own wills. It is not our "wisdom" or desires that must prevail. We are subject to Christ and focused on service to others, who are also forgiven sinners.

Only Christ is wise. Let us think of ourselves in the right way.

6 2

We Are All Lazarus

We are all Lazarus before God. The rich man, too, is
Lazarus. He is the poor leper before God. And only
when we know that we are all Lazarus, because we all
live through the mercy of God, do we see Lazarus in
our brother. (11:449)

⌐⌐⌐

J esus' parable of the rich man and Lazarus tells us of a rich
man who had a poor man, Lazarus, laying at his gate,
covered with sores and in desperate need of food. When both
died, the rich man found that he was tormented in Hades. In
his lifetime he had done nothing to relieve the pain of Lazarus,
who was at his gate. The poor beggar Lazarus exposed the
poverty of the rich man. The rich man paid no attention to
the one who was in need.

Bonhoeffer commented in a sermon, "We are all Lazarus
before God. The rich man, too, is Lazarus. He is the poor
leper before God. And only when we know that we are all
Lazarus, because we all live through the mercy of God, do
we see Lazarus in our brother."

Those among us who are blessed with material possessions and power are as poor as the beggar Lazarus. We all

live through the mercy of God. Nothing we have or gain in this life as material possessions, abilities, or capacities can relieve us from our spiritual state of being in need of God's everlasting mercy.

Only when we recognize that we are all Lazarus in the presence of God and see our own need before God, Bonhoeffer maintained, will we be able to see Lazarus in other people. When we see we are all beggars, we will care for others and meet their needs. "We are all Lazarus"—help us!

6 3

Confession of Sins

What does confession mean? To open yourself to Jesus
Christ with all your sins, weaknesses, vices, suffering, and, on the strength of his word, to give him your
whole heart without the slightest reservation. (16:501)

⌐⌐⌐

What does it mean to be a "whole person" or a "healthy
person"? How can we have fullness of life?

Bonhoeffer addressed this in an essay, "The Best
Physician" (1941). He said wholeness and health and newness
of life can happen simply—but in a way that penetrates to the
depths of our lives. New life comes through confession that is
genuine and forgiveness of all our sins by God.

Bonhoeffer explained, "What does confession mean? To
open yourself to Jesus Christ with all your sins, weaknesses,
vices, suffering, and, on the strength of his word, to give him
your whole heart without the slightest reservation."

Confession of sins goes to the core of our existence. In
confession we let go of our desires to control ourselves and
give up our whole selves—all our sins and rebellions against
God, and our failures to live as God desires. We let go of self-
justifications for our actions. We lay all things before God

and ask for divine forgiveness, with our whole hearts, and no reservations: "Have mercy on me, O God" (Psalm 51:1).

In forgiveness, God obliterates our entire unholy past, our bungled actions, and speaks a word of power: "Forgiven." A new, joyful life begins!

God forgives us through Jesus Christ. Christ is the best and only physician. He knows us in our depths, takes our sins upon himself, and carries them to the cross. Jesus is our savior. He heals our hearts, bodies, and souls.

Jesus heals and gives us the best healing: salvation. This is the new life. Will we receive it?

64

Trusting the Holy Spirit

The Holy Spirit is not a lifeless word on a page but the living God [2 Corinthians 3:6]. Thus the church-community can entrust itself to the Holy Spirit in every decision and firmly believe that the Holy Spirit is present and works up and in it, and does not let us stumble along in the dark as long as we only and earnestly wish to hear the Spirit's teaching. (15:555)

⌒⌒⌒

Every year the church celebrates the Day of Pentecost. We rejoice that God's Holy Spirit came upon the church, empowering it to live as a "community of the Spirit," and that the church is forever united with God in Jesus Christ (Acts 2).

"The Spirit gives life," said Paul (2 Corinthians 3:6). Over and over, the Spirit brings new life through faith in Jesus Christ. The Spirit abides with Jesus' disciples in the church community. Bonhoeffer preached that this means the church can "entrust itself to the Holy Spirit in every decision and firmly believe that the Holy Spirit is present and works up and in it, and does not let us stumble along in the dark as long as we only and earnestly wish to hear the Spirit's teaching."

What a comfort and joy the Holy Spirit brings! The Spirit leads and guides the church, helping us all along the way. We listen for the Spirit's teaching to give us direction for what God wants the church to be and to do in every situation (John 14:26). We are not left on our own to determine the church's direction—or our own direction in life. We can trust the Spirit!

Are we listening to hear the Spirit's teaching? Are we trusting God's Spirit to lead us into paths of mission and ministry? Trust the Holy Spirit!

6 5

Wagering Your Life on God's Word

Faith exists when I yield myself to God, [to the extent that] I will wager my life on God's Word, even and especially there where it goes against all visible appearances. Only when I give up having visible confirmation do I believe in God. The only guarantee that faith can bear is the Word of God itself. (12:358)

⌐⌐⌐

Mark Twain famously said that "faith is believing something you know ain't true." For many, this is the character of faith. We prefer believing in things we can scientifically "prove" or see with our own eyes.

But biblical faith is different. Faith in God is being willing to entrust one's self to God. God is the one who calls us, whose Word we believe, and to whom we are willing to give our lives to obey. Bonhoeffer described the nature of faith in his lectures on Christology. According to student notes, he said, "Faith exists when I yield myself to God, [to the extent that] I will wager my life on God's Word, even and especially there where it goes against all visible appearances. Only when I give up having visible confirmation do I believe in God. The only guarantee that faith can bear is the Word of God itself."

We wager our lives on God—"even and especially" when we do not have "visible confirmation." We cannot "prove God" as we prove something in a scientific experiment. Faith is "conviction of things not seen" (Hebrews 11:1). Faith means trust. We trust God's Word to us—simply because it is God's Word! We believe fully and completely, giving up all means of trying to "prove" faith. We "bet our life" on God's Word, our only "guarantee" being that it is "the Word of God itself." Only this is faith!

6 6

One Day and the Next Day

One day is long enough to keep one's faith; the next day
will have its own worries. (5:78)

⌒⌒⌒

We think of faith in Jesus Christ as a long-term commitment of our lives. This is exactly right. We live by faith
as a basic trust in Christ, for forgiveness of our sins and for
leading us into ways of discipleship and service.

But faith is also a renewed commitment, day by day. In
one sense, faith is "new every morning" (Lamentations 3:23).

Bonhoeffer speaks of a day's work coming to an end and
our thankfulness to God. Our hearts are filled with gladness.
All the worries of the day can be put away, entrusted to the
grace and goodness of God.

Worry is part of our lives. We worry about many things
every day. Our only antidote to worry is faith. We turn our
worries over to the God, in whom we trust. Jesus said, "So do
not worry about tomorrow, for tomorrow will bring worries
of its own. Today's trouble is enough for today" (Matthew
6:34). This is a background for Bonhoeffer's comment, "One
day is long enough to keep one's faith; the next day will have
its own worries."

When we turn our worries over to God, we are grateful for this day, and we entrust our next day—with all its anxieties and worries—to God. If "today's trouble is enough for today," then so is our faith sufficient for today...and tomorrow! Martin Luther once advised his wife, Katie, to pray and let God worry. That's good advice for us. Our faith is renewed every day. We entrust each day to God, and we entrust all our tomorrows to God as well. We let God "worry" for us!

67

Discerning the Will of God

> The will of God...is not a system of rules that are fixed
> from the outset, but always new and different in each
> different life circumstance. This is why it is necessary to
> discern again and again what the will of God is. (6:321)

⌁⌁⌁

One of our ongoing needs is to know the will of God for
our lives. Day by day we trust and seek to know and do
what God wants of us.

Knowing the will of God is an act of discernment. We do
not "automatically" know what God wants of us or in what
directions our lives should go. Through Scripture reading,
prayer, and consultation with others we try—by faith—to
understand God's will.

This is an ongoing process. Our perceptions of God's will
can change over time as we develop, as our circumstances
are altered, and as our contexts change. We always need
our minds renewed so we "may discern what is the will of
God" (Romans 12:2). Bonhoeffer wrote, "The will of God
... is not a system of rules that are fixed from the outset, but
always new and different in each different life circumstance.

This is why it is necessary to discern again and again what the will of God is."

Our Christian lives are exciting because we never know what God's will may mean for us! God's Spirit is always at work and active in leading us into God's ways. We are "transformed" by the "renewing of our minds" and continually transformed as God's will becomes real for us in new and important ways. There are dynamic opportunities before us to do the will of God. These are waiting to be discerned. Our constant prayer is to be open and sensitive to God's Spirit leading us into God's ways for us!

6 8

Being United with God's Will

A person's strength comes solely from being united
with the will of God. (16:350)

〜〜〜

In 1938, Bonhoeffer confirmed Maximilian von Wedemeyer.
Four years later, on August 22, 1942, Wedemeyer's father,
Hans von Wedemeyer, captain of a cavalry regiment, was
killed at Stalingrad. On August 24, Bonhoeffer wrote in a
letter to Maximilian that "a person's strength comes solely
from being united with the will of God."

This comment came in the context of military action. But
it is a true expression for our own lives and commitments
as Christians. Jesus was dedicated to doing the will of God
throughout his ministry. At the end, just hours before his
death, Jesus prayed to God in the Garden of Gethsemane:
"If you are willing, remove this cup from me; yet not my will
but yours be done" (Luke 22:42). Jesus accepted God's will,
which led to his crucifixion.

It is a natural human desire and reaction to turn away
from impending suffering. Jesus united himself with the will
of God, which led to his suffering and death—but also to
salvation for humanity through his death on the cross. Jesus'

strength did not come from his own willpower or resolve. It came from his unity with God's will. This was what gave Jesus power to endure. Bonhoeffer shared this conviction from prison, where he awaited the unknown that could—and did—lead to his death.

In all things, like Jesus and Bonhoeffer, we find that when we pray "Not my will but yours be done," we gain true strength, which can see us through any difficulty in life. Being committed to God's will is our greatest comfort. We are united with God's purposes. God's presence and strength sustains us. "Thy will be done."

6 9

God's Way in the World

God's way in the world leads onto the cross and through
the cross to life. For this reason do not be alarmed, do
not be afraid—be faithful! But what does being faithful mean here other than standing and falling with the
word of Christ, with his preaching of the kingdom of
peace, than knowing that despite everything Christ's
words are stronger than all the powers of evil? (11:426)

⌐⌐⌐

When Bonhoeffer preached on Matthew 24:6-14 in
Berlin on February 21, 1932, social and economic
problems abounded, and Hitler, communist, and socialist
movements were very active. Bonhoeffer foresaw suffering
ahead for the church. He believed Christians were called by
Jesus to be people of peace. He believed the church was being
called to follow Christ on the way to the cross.

"God's way in the world leads onto the cross and through
the cross to life," preached Bonhoeffer. The suffering Christ
calls disciples to follow him in this path. Yet, "do not be
afraid—be faithful!" said Bonhoeffer. Being faithful means
"standing and falling with the word of Christ, with his
preaching of the kingdom of peace." The word of Christ is

what the church—and each Christian—is to follow. This word is Jesus' preaching of the kingdom of peace. God's way in the world is suffering, especially for peace—which is God's desire for the human family. For God is "the God of peace" (Romans 15:33). As events in Germany developed, Bonhoeffer's commitment to peace became stronger.

The way of the cross leads to life. "Despite everything," Bonhoeffer proclaimed, "Christ's words are stronger than all the powers of evil." This faith sustains through the cross and beyond. This conviction is ours as well. We proclaim God's "kingdom of peace" in the face of all powers of evil.

7 0

In Step with God

> But all this has its time and the main thing is that
> we remain in step with God and not keep rushing a
> few steps ahead, though also not lagging a single step
> behind either. (8:228–29)

~~~

There's a line from an old song: "This world is not my home, I'm just a-passin' through."

We know we will not permanently reside in this world. We are born, and we die. As Ecclesiastes says, "For everything there is a season" (Ecclesiastes 3:1). All earthly things blossom and fade; all is temporary. So in one sense, as Christians, we do look beyond the present to the eternal future God promises us in Jesus Christ.

But, as an old saying warns, we don't want to be "so heavenly minded that we are no earthly good!" We don't want to look beyond the present life in such a single-minded way that we miss what God is doing in the here and now!

Bonhoeffer cautioned on this when he wrote, "But all this has its time and the main thing is that we remain in step with God and not keep rushing a few steps ahead, though also not lagging a single step behind either." We are to live "in step with God."

We like to set our own timetables and agendas. We like God to meet these! But Ecclesiastes also says that God has "made everything suitable for its time" (Ecclesiastes 3:11). Our life now is to be in step with God—not trying to force God to slow down or to act more quickly.

We know what it is like sometimes to ask, "Why doesn't God hurry?" Or to say, "Slow down, God, you're going to fast!" Instead, we need to trust God's time, not our own. Keep in step with God!

7 1

When God Is Closest

> Those who have found God in the cross of Jesus Christ
> know how wondrously God is concealed in this world
> and how in fact God is closest to us precisely when
> we think God is farthest away. Those of us who have
> found God in the cross will also forgive all our enemies
> because God has forgiven us. (14:853)

⇌⇌⇌

The cross is the central symbol of Christianity. On the cross, Jesus Christ died for the sins of the world. It looked like his death was pure folly, foolishness—how could this death have any power or meaning?

But the "message about the cross" reveals the "power of God," said Paul (1 Corinthians 1:18). God's "weakness is stronger than human strength" (1:25).

Bonhoeffer said,

> Those who have found God in the cross of Jesus Christ
> know how wondrously God is concealed in this world
> and how in fact God is closest to us precisely when
> we think God is farthest away. Those of us who have

found God in the cross will also forgive all our enemies because God has forgiven us.

This is God's amazing work! God is hidden in the cross of Jesus, so the world cannot know Christ—except by the faith God gives. God is concealed and hidden from view, but is actually closest to us "precisely when we think God is farthest away." We would not think a crucified person could bring God close to us. But Jesus' cross makes God present to us—through Jesus' suffering and death. When we think God is farthest from us—when we suffer and are in deepest need—God is with us in the suffering of God's Son. God forgives us in the cross. This means we can now forgive others, even our enemies. Will we?

7 2

When Life Is Smashed Against the Rocks

> Where a life is smashed against the rocks of reality, the
> light of divine help suddenly shines forth. Just when the
> sea is storming most furiously during the night, the sun
> rises. God does not want to be where human beings
> are trying to be great. Where human beings seem to be
> sinking in darkness, there God establishes the kingdom
> of divine glory and love. (10:526)

⌐⌐⌐

There are times when our lives seem to be smashed against
the rocks. We face dangerous circumstances, the most
difficult problems. On all sides there is no hope. We see no
way to help ourselves. Reality brings the hard rocks that
threaten to smash us into despair and ruin.

Then, says Bonhoeffer, "the light of divine help suddenly
shines forth." God comes to help and to meet us at the low-
est point we can imagine. For "just when the sea is storm-
ing most furiously during the night, the sun rises." God's
constancy continues. God's help meets us at the point of our
greatest need. No human aid can do what the divine assis-
tance can do for us. Then we experience for ourselves, what

Paul learned from God: "'My grace is sufficient for you, for power is made perfect in weakness'" (2 Corinthians 12:9).

This is what we experience in all dimensions of our lives. We cannot be self-sufficient, or even try to be! Bonhoeffer wrote that "God does not want to be where human beings are trying to be great." When we seek greatness, there is no room for God. Instead, "where human beings seem to be sinking in darkness, there God establishes the kingdom of divine glory and love." God's powerful glory and love does for us what we cannot do for ourselves—saves us!

7 3

Stammering Prayer

As helpful as the church's tradition of prayer is for learning how to pray, nevertheless it cannot take the place of the prayer that I owe to my God today. Here the poorest stammering can be better than the best-phrased prayer. (5:71)

～～～

Many things in life must be experienced before we can really say we have done them. We can read a driver's manual for driving a car. But ultimately we have to get behind the wheel and drive. We want airplane pilots to have masterful theoretical knowledge about how to fly their planes. But we also want to be sure they have logged many hours of actual flight time before we are comfortable buckling our safety belts.

So too with prayer. Bonhoeffer wrote, "As helpful as the church's tradition of prayer is for learning how to pray, nevertheless it cannot take the place of the prayer that I owe to my God today. Here the poorest stammering can be better than the best-phrased prayer."

Bonhoeffer warned that using "ecclesial forms" and set prayers can become an evasion of genuine prayer. We may know "how" to pray, but that does not take the place of actually praying to God. We are obliged to pray, and we must experience prayer—by praying!

Perhaps we feel our prayers are not adequate. If we are addressing God, does God expect "perfect prayers"? Fortunately, we are assured this is not the case. Paul wrote that "the Spirit helps us in our weakness; for we do not know how to pray as we ought, but that very Spirit intercedes with sighs too deep for words" (Romans 8:26). The Spirit helps us! When our prayers are genuinely offered to God in faith, our poorest stammering efforts receive the interceding action of the Spirit. Praise God!

7 4

Silence

> We are silent early in the morning because God should
> have the first word, and we are silent before going to
> bed because the last word also belongs to God....In
> the end silence means nothing other than waiting for
> God's Word and coming from God's Word with a bless-
> ing. (5:85)

⌒⌒⌒

We live in a noisy world. Noise, noise, all around! Where is silence in our lives? Times of silence are important. They help us focus on realities beyond whatever our ears are barraged with at the present time.

Bonhoeffer wrote, "We are silent early in the morning because God should have the first word, and we are silent before going to bed because the last word also belongs to God....In the end silence means nothing other than waiting for God's Word and coming from God's Word with a blessing."

Do we practice silence when we arise in the morning? Do we listen to God's Word before we attend to human words?

Do we practice silence before going to bed? Do we let God have the last word in our consciousness before entrusting ourselves to God in sleep?

Silence is the time we wait for God's Word and are blessed by God's Word. The psalmist wrote, "For God alone my soul waits in silence; from him comes my salvation" (Psalm 62:1). When we know salvation comes from God, we wait and listen to receive God's Word to us.

Again, the psalmist says, "For God alone my soul waits in silence, for my hope is from him" (Psalm 62:5). Our hope comes not from the sounds around us, whatever they are. Our hope is in God and in the salvation God gives us now in Jesus Christ and forevermore.

Practice silence, morning and night. Wait for God in silence and be blessed!

75

Gratitude

Gratitude is just another word for the faith that remains unshaken even when God seems to be concealed for a short moment, faith that is joyous amid tears because it knows about Christ the redeemer, has its foundation completely in Christ, and holds fast to his good news. (10:578)

⁓⁓⁓

Life can be difficult. Tragedies occur. Sadnesses descend upon us. Even God can seem far away or hidden from us. How do we hold on? Where is our help?

Paul's words speak to feelings like these: "Rejoice always, pray without ceasing, give thanks in all circumstances; for this is the will of God in Christ Jesus for you" (1 Thessalonians 5:16-18). Through it all, Paul urges us to continue to give thanks, rejoice, and pray. These are basics of the Christian life, which can sustain us.

Bonhoeffer saw these sentiments focused in the word *gratitude*. He preached, "Gratitude is just another word for the faith that remains unshaken even when God seems to be concealed for a short moment, faith that is joyous amid tears because it knows about Christ the redeemer, has its foundation completely in Christ, and holds fast to his good news."

We can be grateful in the midst of the toughest times of life because gratitude expresses faith. When God seems far away, we can be grateful; we believe God is with us, even when it is difficult to perceive God's presence. We can be grateful through our tears in life because Jesus Christ is our redeemer. Christ is the sure foundation who sustains us and who we recognize by faith.

Gratitude expresses faith. We have faith in the gospel of Jesus Christ. That faith is expressed in our gratitude to the God who loves us, redeems us, and is always with us in Jesus Christ!

7 6

Don't Go to Bed Unreconciled

When night falls, the true light of God's Word shines
brighter for the community of faith....It is a decisive
rule of every Christian community that every division
that the day has caused must be healed in the evening.
It is perilous for the Christian to go to bed with an
unreconciled heart. (5:78–79)

⌒⌒⌒

In "The Day Together" in *Life Together*, Bonhoeffer wrote
about the night and the experience of God when we ask
for God's blessing, peace, and preservation for others. We
entrust ourselves to God's power and recognize God works
even when we are tired.

But nighttime is also a time for Christian forgiveness.
Bonhoeffer recounts an old custom in monasteries, when the
abbot asked the brothers to forgive him for his sins against
them. When he is assured of their forgiveness, they likewise
ask for the abbot's forgiveness of their sins. They practiced
Paul's injunction, "Do not let the sun go down on your anger"
(Ephesians 4:26).

Then Bonhoeffer writes, "It is a decisive rule of every
Christian community that every division that the day has

caused must be healed in the evening. It is perilous for the Christian to go to bed with an unreconciled heart."

These words speak to us, no matter where we find ourselves in the evening. Sins and slights and malicious actions must be forgiven before one closes one's eyes in sleep. Going to bed with "an unreconciled heart" is perilous because any evening, one may close one's eyes for the last time, in death. Living or dying with an unreconciled heart is dangerous anytime.

Reconciliation is central to the gospel, where God has reconciled us in Jesus Christ (2 Corinthians 5:19). So we must be reconciled with others each and every day. Be reconciled before bedtime!

7 7

God Loves Our Enemies

> The cross is not the private property of any human
> being, but it belongs to all human beings; it is valid for
> all human beings. God loves our enemies—this is what
> the cross tells us. He suffers for their sake; he experi-
> ences misery and pain for their sake; he has given his
> dear Son for them. Everything depends on this; that
> whenever we meet an enemy, we immediately think:
> this is someone whom God loves; God has given every-
> thing for him. (15:467–68)

━━━

The cross of Jesus Christ is no one's "private property,"
proclaimed Bonhoeffer in a sermon on January 23, 1938.
It's easy to think it may be—"Jesus died for me." That's true.
But there's more: the cross is "valid for all human beings,"
Bonhoeffer said.

That "all" includes even our enemies. Jesus commanded
us to "love your enemies" (Matthew 5:44). This has been
called the hardest command of all to follow. Paul underlined
our need to help our enemies (Romans 12:20).

Bonhoeffer reminds us of why we should live this way.
God loves our enemies. "This is what the cross tells us," he

said. God has given God's own Son to "experience misery and pain" for our enemies. This is what we should think when we meet an enemy: God loves you. God has given Jesus—for you.

Bonhoeffer went on to put it succinctly. Remember you were God's enemy. God gave you mercy without your deserving it. This means for you to remember that God went to the cross in Jesus Christ for your enemy. God loves your enemy, even as God loves you.

These are hard words to hear and obey. God's love comes to us. But God's love extends beyond us to those who are enemies to us. Love your enemies—God does!

7 8

Bread Is from God's Grace

We cannot simply take it for granted that our own
work provides us with bread; rather this is God's order
of grace. The day belongs to God alone. (5:77)

～～～

W e are used to thinking that when we work hard, we
get results. This conviction drives our days. We work
and achieve...and receive the benefits. In most of life, this is
the natural way things work. So we push ourselves—and our
children—into this way of thinking.

When it comes to the necessities of life, such as "our daily
bread," do we recognize there is another dimension at work
here?

Bonhoeffer reminds us that ultimately, it is God who
feeds us. We can never merit the "bread" we need to sustain
life. When we eat a meal, we see before us the expression of
God's grace and faithfulness. God is preserving and guiding
our lives by providing for our basic human need: the need
to eat. We receive the good gifts of God with thanksgiving.
Bonhoeffer writes, "We cannot simply take it for granted that
our own work provides us with bread; rather this is God's
order of grace. The day belongs to God alone."

It is no wonder that in his model prayer for his disciples—and for us—Jesus instructs us to express this dependence on God for our basic needs for life: "Give us this day our daily bread" (Matthew 6:11). God provides for us daily, as God had done for the Israelites in the desert by giving manna for the people to eat (Numbers 11:7-9). We live by faith, day by day, depending on God's grace to enable our lives to continue. "The day belongs to God alone," says Bonhoeffer. Give thanks to God: "Thank you for the food we eat!"

7 9

Divine Rainbow of Peace

The peace of God is God's loyalty despite our own disloyalty. In the peace of God we are secure, protected,
and loved. Admittedly, God does not completely elimi-
nate our care, our responsibility, our unrest, but behind
all this bustle and worry, the divine rainbow of peace
has risen, and we find our lives supported and in unity
with the eternal life of God. (10:549)

〜〜〜

A great quest for many people is to find inner peace. What
will comfort and sustain us, even through difficult days?
What can make us secure within ourselves to face life? In a
disturbing world, where is peace found?

Bonhoeffer speaks of the peace of God in our quotation.
This peace is given by God and is "God's loyalty despite our
own disloyalty." This is comforting in itself! "In the peace
of God," Bonhoeffer told his congregation, "we are secure,
protected, and loved" (Philippians 4:7). God's peace can sustain us.

God's peace upholds us but does not "completely elimi-
nate our care, our responsibility, our unrest." In other words,
God's peace does not bring us to what the old folk song

describes: "where never is heard a discouraging word, and the skies are not cloudy all day." We have cares and troubles, and we have to take action—God's peace does not relieve us of responsibilities.

Yet there is a promise. Bonhoeffer says, "Behind all this bustle and worry, the divine rainbow of peace has risen, and we find our lives supported and in unity with the eternal life of God." This is just what we need! In and through all our difficulties and worries, there is a divine rainbow of peace. This gives hope. We see it and sense it. God supports our lives by bringing us into "unity with the eternal life of God." Peace!

Our Lives with Others

8 0

Seeing Outstretched Hands

> To abide in love means to have open eyes, to be able
> to see something that only a few see, namely, the out-
> stretched, begging hands of the others who are along
> the way, and now not be able to do anything less but
> to act, to help, to do one's duty, using everything one
> has. That may be here or there. More important is that,
> wherever it is, one can always allow oneself to be inter-
> rupted by God.(11:442)

⸺⸺⸺

We like to live, following our own agendas and desires. We resist interruptions, things that put us "behind schedule" or upset our plans.

But people who love according to God's love in Jesus Christ must always "sit loose" with our own timetables. We must allow ourselves to be interrupted by God. First John reminds us that "God is love, and those who abide in love abide in God, and God abides in them" (1 John 4:16). To abide in God is to abide in love, which is to be expressed in very practical ways to others.

Bonhoeffer preached on May 12, 1932, in Berlin on Pentecost Sunday. He told the congregation,

To abide in love means to have open eyes, to be able to see something that only a few see, namely, the outstretched, begging hands of the others who are along the way, and now not be able to do anything less but to act, to help, to do one's duty, using everything one has. That may be here or there. More important is that, wherever it is, one can always allow oneself to be interrupted by God.

When outstretched, begging hands of those in need reach out to us, we can only act, help, and use everything we have to bring relief. Will we see the "outstretched, begging hands"?

8 1

Our Neighbor's Need

It would be blasphemy against God and our neighbor to leave the hungry unfed while saying that God is closest to those in deepest need. We break bread with the hungry and share our home with them for the sake of Christ's love, which belongs to the hungry as much as it does to us.... To bring bread to the hungry is preparing the way for the coming of grace. (6:163)

⌐⌐⌐

God meets us through the needs of our neighbor. This is a biblical truth dramatically demonstrated in Jesus' parable of the judgment of the nations (Matthew 25:31-46). In the parable, the basis of judgment was how one has responded to the needs of those who were hungry, strangers, unclothed, sick, and in prison (25:42-43). This same theme was part of the message of the prophet Isaiah in the Old Testament. What God genuinely desires for people is "to share your bread with the hungry, and bring the homeless poor into your house; when you see the naked, to cover them" (Isaiah 58:7). These are direct, practical actions that show the genuineness of one's faith.

Bonhoeffer clearly summarized the meaning of God's desires when he wrote:

> It would be blasphemy against God and our neighbor to leave the hungry unfed while saying that God is closest to those in deepest need. We break bread with the hungry and share our home with them for the sake of Christ's love, which belongs to the hungry as much as it does to us.... To bring bread to the hungry is preparing the way for the coming of grace.

When we meet the needs of others for the sake of Christ's love, we are doing what God desires. We are, said Bonhoeffer, "preparing the way for the coming of grace"—God's work indeed!

8 2

Christ Leads Us to Serve Each Other

The Christ who governs us leads us to serve each other.
(1:141)

⌐⌐⌐

Paul speaks of the church as the body of Christ (see 1 Corinthians 12:27). Each congregation is part of the full body of Christ. As individual Christians, we are "members of his body" (Ephesians 5:30; Romans 12:5). In the church, we live and work together as a community. We put into daily action what it means to be part of the fellowship of believers through which God is at work in the world, in Christ, by the power of the Holy Spirit.

As members of the body of Christ, we exist by the power of Christ. We look to Jesus Christ as "the head of the body, the church" (Colossians 1:18). Christ is above us and before us, calling the church into existence and governing the church by his Spirit as "the church-community."

Bonhoeffer recognized Christ as the head of the church. He wrote that "the Christ who governs us leads us to serve each other." The image of the church as the body of Christ is a "functional" image. That is, the body exists to do something! Its purpose is to obey and serve Jesus Christ. We do this when we serve each other. This is the church's mission. This is how the church shows to whom it belongs, by doing what Christ wants in this world. Members of the body of Christ serve each other and serve the world. As 1 Peter puts it, "Serve one another with whatever gift each of you has received" (1 Peter 4:10).

An old expression says, "We are saved to serve; not saved to sit." We serve others in the most loving and radical ways possible because this is the will of Christ for his body.

8 3

Burden Bearing

As Christ bears our burdens, so we are to bear the
burden of our sisters and brothers. The law of Christ,
which must be fulfilled, is to bear the cross. (4:88)

⸚⸚⸚

Burdens in life come in all forms, shapes, and sizes. We
know that all too well!

We can be burdened by more things than we can imagine.
Think of all your anxieties, the difficulties and problems that
have been your companions through the years! We remember, and we know our burdens have had to be carried.

We also know the burdens of others. They have problems
too. Some of these can be shared; others can only be borne
alone—with the help of Jesus Christ.

Jesus is the great "burden-bearer." He promises, "Come
to me, all you that are weary and are carrying heavy burdens,
and I will give you rest" (Matthew 11:28). He is our comfort
and our hope. Jesus bore the sin of the whole world, even as
it led him to die on the cross.

But Jesus asks us to share burdens—to bear the burdens
of others. As Paul said, "Bear one another's burdens, and in
this way you will fulfill the law of Christ" (Galatians 6:2).

Bonhoeffer wrote: "As Christ bears our burdens, so we are to bear the burden of our sisters and brothers. The law of Christ, which must be fulfilled, is to bear the cross."

We enter into the lives of others and carry their burdens with them because this is what God has done for us in Jesus Christ. We "bear the cross"—all the sadnesses, sorrows, and distresses of our sisters and brothers—as ways of sharing the love of Christ, which led him to the cross for us. As we follow Jesus, let us bear others' burdens.

8 4

Listening Instead of Talking

> Many people seek a sympathetic ear and do not find it
> among Christians, because these Christians are talking
> even when they should be listening. But Christians who
> can no longer listen to one another will soon no longer
> be listening to God either; they will always be talking
> even in the presence of God. (5:98)

～～～

Every day of our lives, we talk and listen. These form the
rhythms of our lives. They enable conversations and our
interactions with others in meaningful ways. Speaking and
hearing are lifelines in our lives, including our lives of faith.

What are the balances in our lives between speaking and
listening? Which one predominates?

Bonhoeffer considered the ministry of listening to be a
key way of serving others in Christ. But he was concerned
that some Christians talk more than listen. Bonhoeffer wrote,

> Many people seek a sympathetic ear and do not find it
> among Christians, because these Christians are talking
> even when they should be listening. But Christians who
> can no longer listen to one another will soon no longer

be listening to God either; they will always be talking even in the presence of God.

This is an important perspective that can hit home with all of us at various times. We like to talk, to share our opinions. We may even like to prescribe actions others "should take," even when they are most in need of a "sympathetic ear."

We do not realize that listening can serve others better than talking, according to Bonhoeffer. In this he echoes James' injunction: "Let everyone be quick to listen, slow to speak" (James 1:19). We must be quick to listen to others so we can be able to listen to God. Listening to others is what God calls us to do. Are you listening?

8 5

Forgiving Sins Is Required

Forgiving sins is the Christ-suffering required of his disciples. It is required of all Christians. (4:88)

⌐⌐⌐

Our Christian lives are constituted by two dimensions of forgiveness.

First, we are forgiven by God in Jesus Christ. In the hour of his death, as Jesus gasped for breath on the cross, he uttered a prayer on behalf of those who were putting him to death, but also more fully on our behalf as well. Our sin led to Jesus' death. But on the cross, he prayed, "Father, forgive them; for they do not know what they are doing" (Luke 23:34). Our sin is forgiven by God in Christ.

Second, we are commanded to forgive others. As Paul wrote, "Be kind to one another, tenderhearted, forgiving one another, as God in Christ has forgiven you" (Ephesians 4:32). We forgive others because God in Christ has forgiven us.

Bonhoeffer captured these aspects of forgiveness when he wrote, "Forgiving sins is the Christ-suffering required of his disciples. It is required of all Christians." Christ suffered and forgives us. Now, as Jesus' disciples, we enter into the sufferings of Christ by not standing on our "rights" with others, seeking revenge on others, or keeping others indebted to us. No. Now we forgive others!

Forgiving the sins of those who have wronged us is "required of all Christians," said Bonhoeffer. Forgiveness is not an option in the Christian life; it is an absolute necessity. We betray our Lord when we refuse to do for others what Jesus has done for us: forgive!

We realize forgiving others is too difficult for us to do on our own. That's why we must see forgiving as the "Christ-suffering" into which we as Christ's disciples enter. We forgive others by the power of Christ's cross. We are forgiven, so we forgive!

8 6

Entrust Another to God

> From first awakening until our return to sleep, we must commend and entrust the other person to God wholly and without reserve, and let our worries become prayer for the other persons. "With anxieties and with worry …God lets *nothing* be taken from himself." (8:238)

⌐⌐⌐

On Christmas Eve 1943 from his prison cell, Bonhoeffer wrote to his newlywed niece Renate and her husband, Eberhard Bethge. Bonhoeffer had been separated from friends and family for nine months, and the Bethges were facing separation due to Eberhard's military service.

Bonhoeffer wrote of the emptiness of being separated from loved ones. He said he found that while it is possible to cope with the fact of separation, it is magnified when we anticipate the future with worry and anxiety. Then he advised, "From first awakening until our return to sleep, we must commend and entrust the other person to God wholly and without reserve, and let our worries become prayer for the other persons."

Entrusting another to God in all the fullness of their lives is the best antidote to anxiety and worry. When we commend the other's life to God, trusting God to guard, guide, protect, and help them, we can believe. All through the day and all through the night, their times are in God's hands (Psalm 31:15). We can cast all our anxieties for others on God because God cares for them, as well as us (see 1 Peter 5:7). Bonhoeffer said, "We can let our worries become prayer for the other person." When we are tempted to worry, turn the worry over to God as a prayer for another. Bonhoeffer quoted a hymn of Paul Gerhardt, "With anxieties and with worry . . . God lets *nothing* be taken from himself." God holds the other along with all that unsettles us. Entrust others to God!

Love

8 7

Love Matters Most

A human life is only meaningful and worthwhile to the extent that it has love in it, and that a life is nothing, is meaningless and worthless, when it is without love. A life is worth as much as the love in it. Everything else is nothing at all, a matter of indifference, unimportant. All the good and bad, big and little things are unimportant. Only one thing is asked of us—whether we have love. (13:377)

⌒⌒⌒

In October 1934, when Bonhoeffer was a pastor of German Lutherans in London, he preached a series of sermons on 1 Corinthians 13. He said the congregation needed to hear this chapter, especially in light of recent events in Germany, and that the congregation needed to look at itself to hear what it means to love God and love others.

When he preached on 1 Corinthians 13:1-3, Bonhoeffer boldly stated it is love that matters most. Life without love is "nothing." It is "meaningless and worthless." Love gives life value, and "a life is worth as much as the love in it." This captures the essence of what Paul told the Corinthians: if we do not have love, "I am nothing" (v. 2).

Both the "big things" in life and the "little things" in life are unimportant if the essential and most important thing in life is lacking: if we "do not have love" (v. 1). It is hard for us to keep this perspective. We fret and care and try to achieve the things we want, what we think will bring us joy and happiness. But all these are not as important as we think. Life's true meaning is found in love. Make this your focus. In the end, "Only one thing is asked of us—whether we have love." Love matters most!

8 8

Love Wants Everything for Another

Self-love is jealous. It wants something for itself, it wants to win over and possess the other person for itself, *it* wants something from that person. But *love* doesn't want anything *from the* other person—what it wants is everything for that person. It doesn't want to possess the other person, especially not to have him or her jealously all to itself. It only wants to love the other person, because it cannot do otherwise; it only wants the person for his or her own sake. It wants nothing from other people but desires everything for them. (13:383–84)

⌐⌐⌐

There is the greatest difference between "self-love" and "love for another." Bonhoeffer describes self-love as jealous, out for itself, wanting to possess others for our own benefit.

But love for another does not want something "from" another person—"what it wants is everything for that person." It doesn't seek to possess another, to hold someone jealously for our own sake. Love cannot do otherwise than love another. This means we want everything for another, for that person's own sake. Not our own.

Paul's description of love in 1 Corinthians 13:4-7, on which Bonhoeffer's sermon was based, defines love as patient and kind, bearing, hoping, and enduring all things—in relation to another person and for the sake of the other person. We want others to be blessed, to receive all they need, and to know our love for them—a love that comes from God. We do not try to use people for our own benefit. We love them for their own benefit.

In short, says Bonhoeffer, love "wants nothing from other people but desires everything for them." Love is giving and providing for others. This is God's love in Jesus Christ, and this is the love we give others.

8 9

Love Can Stand Anything

Love bears all things—that means it cannot be frightened by any evil. It can look upon and take in all the horror of human sin. It doesn't look away from what is unbearable; it can stand the sight of blood. Love can stand anything. No guilt, no crime, no vice, no disaster is so heavy that love cannot look at it and take it upon itself, for it knows: love is still greater than the greatest guilt. (13:385)

❤❤❤

One of the most amazing descriptions Paul gives about love in 1 Corinthians 13 is that love "bears all things" (v. 7).

We may think there are limits to love. We will love others unless they… We draw lines at certain behaviors, at the things others do to us that are beyond the bounds of what we can love.

But we are called to a love that can stand anything. Bonhoeffer says the love that bears "all things" means love "cannot be frightened by any evil"—no matter what. Even the "horror of human sin" doesn't quench love. Graphically Bonhoeffer says love can "stand the sight of blood." We cannot do this on our own. We cannot love when others treat us horribly. But Bonhoeffer insisted, "No guilt, no crime, no vice, no disaster is so heavy that love cannot look at it and take it upon itself." This kind of love is not within our own power. We know this loving in the face of all horrors is more than we can bear.

But love "bears all things," said Paul. Love can take on all this awfulness. For "love is still greater than the greatest guilt." This is God's love in Christ. God's love can stand anything, even our most evil sin and guilt. We are called to love like that!

9 0

Everything Should Turn into Love

Everything, all our knowledge, insight, thinking, and
talking should in the end move toward and turn into
love. For only what we think because of love, and in
love, will remain, will never end. (13:388)

⌐⌐⌐

We engage life on many levels. We are led into many
duties, activities, interactions, things to think about,
and innumerable conversations with others. Life can be
full—with so much to do!

But where does it all lead? Is there anything that unifies
our lives? Is there any vision or power that pulls together our
various actions to give overall purpose or direction?

When Bonhoeffer preached on 1 Corinthians 13:8-12, he
noted Paul's promise that "love never ends." Love lasts. Love
is eternal. Love is the power that can bring all things together.
Love should be the goal of all we do. Love is our purpose for
living. Bonhoeffer proclaimed to his London congregation,
"Everything, all our knowledge, insight, thinking, and talking should in the end move toward and turn into love. For
only what we think because of love, and in love, will remain,
will never end."

This gives us something to consider, doesn't it? Can we envision our lives—in all their many dimensions and activities—as constantly being turned toward love and into love? Is love our dominant verb? What if we asked ourselves about everything we think or say or do: Does this express love? How would, or could, our lives be different?

It is through love that God acts in us. God enables us to love. As 1 John puts it, "Love is from God" (1 John 4:7). "Love never ends," said Paul (1 Corinthians 13:8). Love remains when all else is gone. Love is our legacy. All we are and all we do should turn into love!

9 1

Love Stays Its Course

Because love is God's very self and God's will; that is why it never ends, it never doubts, it stays its course. It pursues its way with sure steps, like a sleepwalker, straight through the midst of all the dark places and perplexities of this world. It goes down into the depths of human misery and up to the heights of human splendor. It goes out to enemies as well as to friends, and it never abandons anyone, even when it is abandoned by everyone. Love follows after its beloved through guilt and disgrace and loneliness, all of which are not part of it; it is simply there and never ends. And it blesses every place it enters. (13:388)

〜〜〜

Love is central to the Christian life because love expresses God's very self and God's will. God is eternal, so love is eternal. "Love never ends" (1 Corinthians 13:8). Love is at the core of our Christian lives.

Like God, love stays its course. Bonhoeffer says God's love is "like a sleepwalker." Love walks right into all the "dark places and perplexities of this world." Love does not turn away from difficulties. "It goes down into the depths of human misery and up to the heights of human splendor." In good times and bad, love persistently walks through life with us. Love "goes out to enemies as well as to friends, and it never abandons anyone, even when it is abandoned by everyone." This is difficult—to love enemies and abandon no one. Love pursues through guilt, disgrace, and loneliness. No matter what, love keeps on loving!

As we live love, we will find that love "blesses every place it enters." May our love bless every person and situation. Live knowing that love "stays its course" and never ends!

9 2

Love the Child of God in Our Neighbor

> God loved human beings in Jesus Christ, made them
> into children of God while they were yet sinners. Let
> us love the child of God in our neighbor, even if that
> person makes a mistake, even if that person falls. In
> our neighbor, we love God; that is the great gift of
> Christianity. (10:499)

~~~

In Barcelona on June 24, 1928, Bonhoeffer preached on
Jesus' words in Matthew 7:1: "Do not judge, so that you
may not be judged." This sermon emphasized that judging
others destroys community, especially a church community.
But when we pardon, love, and intercede for others, our community is built up.

Bonhoeffer saw a chain reaction here. Judging others creates arrogance and self-righteousness. This arrogance leads
to separation, alienation, and hostility among people in the
community. But love creates humility and trust in God's com-
passion. Humility leads to unity and friendship. This is ultimately possible because love comes from God.

Bonhoeffer urged the congregation to remember that
"God loved human beings in Jesus Christ, made them into

children of God while they were yet sinners" (Romans 5:8). So, Bonhoeffer continued: "Let us love the child of God in our neighbor, even if that person makes a mistake, even if that person falls. In our neighbor, we love God; that is the great gift of Christianity."

This is the practical expression of the theological conviction of God's love for humanity in Jesus Christ so that even as sinners, they are "children of God." This unites each of us with the whole human family. So we love others—even when they make mistakes or fall. This accepting love expresses that we love God "in our neighbor." This love is "the great gift of Christianity."

Let us love one another, even when others fall.

9 3

I Love You in Service to You

I do not love God in the "neighbor," but I love the concrete You; I love the You by placing myself, my entire will, in the service of the You. (1:169)

━ ━ ━

Bonhoeffer's ethics was an ethics of formation. All Christians should be formed and conformed to Jesus Christ. We are to live not by principles and rules but based on Jesus Christ. Jesus frees us to act responsibly in the world as he takes form in the church community and in us. This means we always act concretely, in the here and now. We act in real ways expressing our discipleship, our following Jesus.

When we see Jesus, we see a person who acted in self-giving love and who loved the persons before him. We love others as he commanded (1 John 3:23), and we love "the real neighbor," as Bonhoeffer said. By this he meant we love the person in front of us as a human being whom God calls me to love and who has a claim on me as my neighbor. We love that person. Bonhoeffer wrote, "I do not love God in the 'neighbor,' but I love the concrete You; I love the You by placing myself, my entire will, in the service of the You." This is what Jesus did and what Jesus also commands his disciples to do.

This gives our human relationships special meaning. We are to love as Jesus loved—in his self-giving and sacrifice. We place our entire will in service to the other. We are to be *for* them as Jesus was a person who is *for* us. We love the other with all their needs. God's Spirit gives us power really to love neighbors and to serve them. Love your neighbor!

Living in the World

9 4

Genuine Worldliness Through Christ

The cross of reconciliation sets us free to live before God in the midst of the godless world, sets us free to live in genuine worldliness [*Weltlichkeit*]....A life of genuine worldliness is possible only through the proclamation of the crucified Christ. (6:400–401)

⌐⌐⌐

When we think of the cross of Jesus Christ and the reconciliation and salvation we receive by Christ's work, we know this is the most important and meaningful aspects of our lives. We are now forgiven, set free from the power of sin, and followers of Jesus as his disciples in this world.

Bonhoeffer focuses on where our discipleship takes shape: in the world. Our faith is not a mystical escape from the world; it is the springboard enabling us to dive into the midst of the world as a free person in Jesus Christ (Galatians 5:1).

For Bonhoeffer, "genuine worldliness" comes from our freedom to live before God "in the midst of the godless world." We are free in Christ to love the world God made, to serve others, and to be involved in the full range of life and culture as those liberated from the power of sin. Bonhoeffer showed this in his own life. His advocacy for peace and justice, his political involvements, and his willingness to risk his life for his Christian beliefs showed the depths of the "genuine worldliness" he lived.

This "life of genuine worldliness" is possible "only through the proclamation of the crucified Christ." Christ's cross alone and the liberating reconciliation Christ brings enables this free life of involvement in the world to happen for us. Nothing else releases us to live this way. We fully engage the world through the freedom that comes from the crucified Christ. Now we are immersed in the world. Live here...and now!

9 5

Living Fully in the Midst of Life

If one has completely renounced making something of oneself...then one throws oneself completely into the arms of God, and this is what I call this-worldliness: living fully in the midst of life's tasks, questions, successes and failures, experiences, and perplexities—then one takes seriously no longer one's own sufferings but rather the suffering of God in the world. Then one stays awake with Christ in Gethsemane. And I think this is faith; this is [repentance]. And this is how one becomes a human being, a Christian. (8:486)

⌐⌐⌐

Bonhoeffer's letter to Eberhard Bethge on July 21, 1944, contains his famous comments about the "this-worldliness of life" and Bonhoeffer's conviction that Christianity is a profoundly "this-worldly" faith. Christians are to live the way Jesus lived, as a human being who was fully engaged with life. This is the meaning of faith.

In the quotation above, the complete abandonment of throwing one's self "completely into the arms of God" enables one to "live fully" in "the midst of life's tasks, questions, successes and failure, experiences, and perplexities." Everything life brings us is met by the freedom of belonging to God. We don't take our own sufferings as primary. We are concerned most with "the suffering of God in the world." This suffering is expressed in the suffering of others, as Bonhoeffer often said.

Bonhoeffer uses the image of staying "awake with Christ in Gethsemane," which his disciples were not able to do (Matthew 28:36-46). But we must! This is true faith—"how one becomes a human being, a Christian," said Bonhoeffer. Faith is lived in the midst of life, being fully human and sharing the suffering of God in Jesus Christ as we minister to others in his name. Live fully!

9 6

Treasure Means Idolatry

The heart clings to collected treasure. Stored-up possessions get between me and God. Where my treasure is, there is my trust, my security, my comfort, my God. Treasure means idolatry. (4:162–63)

⌐⌐⌐

All of us have to deal with our possessions. We deal with them in different ways. We acquire them, use them, discard them...and acquire more! This is our cycle of life.

How do we regard our possessions, and what "power" do they have over us? We cannot live without the goods of human life. We must eat and drink and have our basic needs met. So did Jesus. Possessions can be good gifts of God, to bring joy and enable us to live better—for the sake of serving God in Jesus Christ.

Jesus had direct words about possessions: "Do not store up for yourselves treasures on earth...store up for yourselves treasures in heaven....For where your treasure is, there your heart will be also" (Matthew 6:19-21). His blunt conclusion: "You cannot serve God and wealth" (Matthew 6:24). Or, "We cannot serve God and cash!" These words hit us hard. They show us the direction to follow.

Bonhoeffer emphasized that like Israel in the desert where manna was daily given by God (Numbers 11:7-9), so Jesus' disciples should receive what we need daily from God. Bonhoeffer warned, "The heart clings to collected treasure. Stored-up possessions get between me and God. Where my treasure is, there is my trust, my security, my comfort, my God. Treasure means idolatry." When we trust the comforts of "treasure," we cease to trust God, and we worship an idol.

These words caution us. We need "possessions." But we should "sit light" with them. Don't absolutize them. Possessions are God's good gifts to enable us to serve God. Use your "treasure" this way!

9 7

Only the Suffering God Can Help

Only the suffering God can help. (8:479)

⌐⌐⌐

Near the end of his life, as his letters and papers from prison indicate, Bonhoeffer believed what could make Christianity compelling to people who had pushed "God" to the boundaries of their lives instead of at the center, was to realize this: God is a suffering God.

God is with us in the midst of life, including our sufferings. God in Jesus Christ is a "suffering God." Jesus was "pushed out" of this world by dying on a cross. In this he showed that God is weak and that God's "power is made perfect in weakness" (2 Corinthians 12:9). In his weakness and powerlessness, God in Jesus Christ is at our side and helps us. Bonhoeffer cited Matthew 8:17, spoken by Jesus after he had healed Peter's mother-in-law and many in need: "This was to fulfill what had been spoken through the prophet Isaiah, 'He took our infirmities and bore our diseases' [Isaiah 53:4]." Christ helped those people—and us!—not because he is "all-powerful" (omnipotent) but through his own weakness and suffering. God suffers in the world's life, and in Jesus Christ, who suffered, the suffering God helps us.

We can live fully engaged in the world because Jesus suffered in this world and now helps us in our suffering. This is what we need. God is not distant and remote. God is with us in Jesus, who suffers in and with our sufferings. Jesus is the one who is "there" for us. As disciples of Jesus, we follow and share the sufferings of others in this world. We suffer with them because Jesus suffers with us.

God is not far away. God is near to us, always—in Jesus, who shows us the suffering God.

9 8

No Peace Without Truth and Justice

Peace has its boundary in truth and justice. Where truth
and justice are violated there can be no peace. (11:371)

▬▬▬

Bonhoeffer was involved in the work of peace. In July
1932, he participated in a youth peace conference
in Czechoslovakia and gave a lecture where he said peace
between nations was a topic churches needed to address. They
do so on the basis of the authority of Jesus Christ. Christ is
the Lord of the entire world and present in the entire world.
This means the gospel of Christ and Christ's commandments
must be spoken to the concrete situations in the contemporary world. The church must directly address this issue that
emerges from Christ's command: international peace.

In his comment, "Peace has its boundary in truth and
justice. Where truth and justice are violated there can be no
peace," Bonhoeffer identified elements that must go together
for peace among nations to be possible. Against the backdrop
of the "Hitler party," then emerging in Germany, Bonhoeffer's
comment continues to be important for our own times.

A "peace" among nations that is not constituted by "truth
and justice" cannot be stable or long-lasting. It cannot be

true biblical peace. The vision of the psalmist was that under God, "steadfast love and faithfulness will meet; righteousness and peace will kiss each other" (Psalm 85:10). (Hebrew terms here can also be translated "truth" and "justice.") Later, Bonhoeffer would write that the church should be known by this commitment to peace and justice, even more than by its own disciplines to sustain faith and hope.

Even on a personal level, this is true. Peace in human relationships is not possible when truth and justice are violated. When truth and justice are absent, peace cannot be established.

Pray and live for peace—and truth and justice!

9 9

Praying and Doing Justice

We can be Christians today in only two ways, through
prayer and in doing justice among human beings. All
Christian thinking, talking, and organizing must be
born anew, out of that power and action. (8:389)

━━━

In May 1944, Bonhoeffer was in prison. His *Letters and
Papers from Prison* show us his theological thinking during the last period of his life. Bonhoeffer wondered about
Christianity in the midst of a world gone mad with war and
with the secularism that seemed to leave no place for God in
human life.

In "Thoughts on the Day of Baptism of Dietrich Wilhelm
Rüdiger Bethge" (Bonhoeffer's namesake son of his niece
Renate and dear friend, Eberhard Bethge), Bonhoeffer recognized the church's struggle to bring a word of reconciliation and redemption to humankind and to the world. When
the old words lose their power, Bonhoeffer said, "We can
be Christians today in only two ways, through prayer and
in doing justice among human beings. All Christian thinking, talking, and organizing must be born anew, out of that
power and action."

Today, with all we face in the contemporary world, Bonhoeffer's prescription is still important. Prayer and doing justice: these two practices can consume all our energies in ways God wants. We pray to God for the world, the church, and our lives. We do justice, seeking reconciliation, peace, and the establishment of just laws, just practices, and equal justice for all people in society.

We seek new words to speak Christian faith. By Christian action, we express faith in praying and doing justice. We do this in the midst of the world, waiting for God. Bonhoeffer's wish for young Dietrich is a wish for all the faithful: "But the path of the righteous is like the light of dawn, which shines brighter and brighter until full day" (Proverbs 4:18).

1 0 0

God Strengthens Us in Distress

I believe that God can and will let good come out of
everything, even the greatest evil....I believe that in
every moment of distress God will give us as much
strength to resist as we need. But it is not given to us
in advance, lest we rely on ourselves and not on God
alone. (8:46)

⌐⌐⌐

Bonhoeffer's path led through joys and sorrows. His joys
in his family, friends, church, and students were great.
His sufferings and distresses were great also. Bonhoeffer's
imprisonment—charged with plotting against Adolf Hitler—
was his last act of resistance to great evil.

At the turn of the year between 1942 and 1943, Bonhoeffer
wrote about core theological convictions. On the topic of
"Faith on God's Action in History," Bonhoeffer wrote, "I
believe that God can and will let good come out of everything, even the greatest evil....I believe that in every moment
of distress God will give us as much strength to resist as we
need. But it is not given to us in advance, lest we rely on ourselves and not on God alone."

In this testimony of faith in dark days, Bonhoeffer affirms God's providence at work in bringing good out everything that befalls us—even the greatest evils. He echoes Paul's overwhelming confidence that "all things work together for good" (Romans 8:28). We are never left alone. At all times, in "every moment of distress," God is with us, giving us the strength we need to resist the evil we encounter. But strength is not "given to us in advance." We cannot "store strength," like the Israelites in the wilderness trying to hoard the manna God gave anew each morning (Numbers 11). Through it all, in each minute, we do not rely on ourselves but on God.

Timeline of Dietrich Bonhoeffer's Life

1906   February 4: Dietrich Bonhoeffer and twin sister, Sabine, born in Breslau, Germany

1923   Begins theological studies at the University of Tübingen

1927   Defends doctoral dissertation, published as *Sanctorum Communio*

1928   Serves as curate for Lutheran congregation in Barcelona, Spain

1930   Second dissertation completed: *Act and Being*

1930   Studies at Union Theological Seminary in New York City

1931   November 15: Ordained in St. Matthias Church, Berlin

1933   Lectures on Christology at Friedrich Wilhelm University, Berlin

1933   Begins pastorate for German-speaking congregations in London

1935   Opens preacher's seminary of the Confessing Church at Zingst (by the Baltic)

1936   Bonhoeffer's authorization to teach at Friedrich-Wilhelm University, Berlin is withdrawn

1937   September 28: Finkenwalde Seminary closed by Gestapo

1937   Publication of *Discipleship*

1938   Bonhoeffer contacts leaders of the political resistance to Hitler

1939   *Life Together* is published

Timeline of Dietrich Bonhoeffer's Life

1939   Brief trip to Union Theological Seminary but soon returns to Germany

1939   Becomes civilian agent for German Military Intelligence Agency (*Abwehr*)

1940   Prohibited from public speaking and ordered to report regularly to the police

1941   Forbidden to publish due to his "subversive activities"

1943   April 5: Arrested and taken to Tegel prison

1944   July 20: Attempt to assassinate Hitler fails

1944   September 22: Secret files of resistance discovered by Gestapo; Bonhoeffer implicated

1944   October 8: Bonhoeffer moved to prison at the Prinz-Albrecht-Strasse, Berlin

1945   February 7: Transported to Buchenwald concentration camp

1945   April 3: Transported from Buchenwald to Regensburg

1945   April 5: Hitler orders execution of conspirators

1945   April 6: Moved to Schönberg

1945   April 8: Transferred to Flossenbürg concentration camp and court-martialed

1945   April 9: Bonhoeffer executed by hanging; his body burned

Selected Resources for Further Reflection

Primary Sources

Dietrich Bonhoeffer's Works is a seventeen-volume set edited by Victoria J. Barnett and published by Fortress Press. Volumes used in this book are:

Volume 1	*Sanctorum Communio* (2009)
Volume 2	*Act and Being* (1996)
Volume 3	*Creation and Fall* (2004)
Volume 4	*Discipleship* (2001)
Volume 5	*Life Together* and *The Prayerbook of the Bible* (1996)
Volume 6	*Ethics* (2009)
Volume 8	*Letters and Papers from Prison* (2010)
Volume 10	*Barcelona, Berlin, New York 1928–1931* (2008)
Volume 11	*Ecumenical, Academic, and Pastoral Work: 1931–1932* (2012)
Volume 12	*Berlin: 1933* (2009)
Volume 13	*London: 1933–1935* (2007)
Volume 14	*Theological Education at Finkenwalde: 1935–1937* (2013)
Volume 15	*Theological Education Underground: 1937–1940* (2012)
Volume 16	*Conspiracy and Imprisonment: 1940–1945* (2006)
Volume 17	*Indexes and Supplementary Materials* (2014)

Secondary Sources

Bethge, Eberhard. *Dietrich Bonhoeffer: A Biography*. Revised and edited by Victoria J. Barnett. Philadelphia: Fortress, 2000.

de Gruchy, John W., ed. *The Cambridge Companion to Dietrich Bonhoeffer*. New York: Cambridge University Press, 1999.

Haynes, Stephen R. *The Bonhoeffer Legacy: Post-Holocaust Perspectives*. Minneapolis: Fortress, 2006.

———. *The Bonhoeffer Phenomenon: Portraits of a Protestant Saint*. Minneapolis: Fortress, 2004.

Haynes, Stephen R., and Lori Brandt Hale. *Bonhoeffer for Armchair Theologians*. Illustrations by Ron Hill. Louisville: Westminster John Knox, 2009.

Marsh, Charles. *Strange Glory: A Life of Dietrich Bonhoeffer*. New York: Alfred A. Knopf, 2014.

Pugh, Jeffrey. *Religionless Christianity: Dietrich Bonhoeffer in Troubled Times*. New York: T&T Clark, 2008.

Rasmussen, Larry L. *Dietrich Bonhoeffer: Reality and Resistance*. 1972. Reprint, Louisville: Westminster John Knox, 2005.

Schliesser, Christine. *Everyone Who Acts Responsibly Becomes Guilty: Bonhoeffer's Concept of Accepting Guilt*. Louisville: Westminster John Knox, 2008.

DVD

Bonhoeffer: Agent of Grace. Written by Gareth Jones and Eric Till. Directed by Eric Till. Gateway Films: Vision Video, 2000.

Bonhoeffer: Pastor, Pacifist, Nazi Resister. Edited by Matthew B. Kelly and Timothy Finkbiner. Directed by Martin Doblmeier. Journey Films: Bridgestone Multimedia Group, 2003.

Web Resources

Dietrich Bonhoeffer Reading Room
www.tyndale.ca/seminary/mtsmodular/reading-rooms/theology
/bonhoeffer

Dietrich Bonhoeffer—Wikipedia
https://en.wikipedia.org/w/index.php?title=Dietrich_Bonhoeffer
&oldid=818273866

The Bonhoeffer Center
http://thebonhoeffercenter.org/

International Bonhoeffer Society English Language Section
www.dbonhoeffer.org/ibsinfo.htm

About the Author

Dr. Donald K. McKim is an Honorably Retired minister of the Presbyterian Church (U.S.A.). He has served as executive editor for theology for Westminster John Knox Press, a seminary theology professor and academic dean, as well as a pastor.

Dr. McKim is the author and editor of a number of books, including *The Westminster Dictionary of Theological Terms*; *The Authority and Interpretation of the Bible: An Historical Approach* (with Jack B. Rogers); and *Reformation Questions, Reformation Answers: 95 Key Events, People and Issues*. He has also written devotional books, which include *Coffee with Calvin: Daily Devotions*; *Moments with Martin Luther: 95 Daily Devotions*; and *Living into Lent*. His *Sanctuary for Lent 2017* and *Advent: A Calendar of Devotions 2017* were written for the United Methodist Church. He lives with his wife, LindaJo McKim, in Germantown, Tennessee. They have two married children and three grandchildren.

CPSIA information can be obtained
at www.ICGtesting.com
Printed in the USA
LVHW082327120219
607191LV00007B/2/P